IN ONE ARENA

Top Dressage Experts Share
Their Knowledge through the Levels

SHARON BIGGS

HHP

Boonsboro, Maryland

In One Arena

Top Dressage Experts Share
Their Knowledge through the Levels

©2001 Sharon Biggs

Published in the United States of America by
Half Halt Press, Inc.
P.O. Box 67
Boonsboro, MD 21713
www.halfhaltpress.com

Book and jacket design by Design Point.
Editorial services by Samantha Harrison.

Library of Congress Cataloging-in-Publication Data

In one arena: top dressage experts share their knowledge through the levels / [edited by] Sharon Biggs.
    p. cm.
  ISBN 0-939481-60-X
   1. Dressage. I. Title: In 1 arena. II. Biggs, Sharon, 1966- III. Title.

SF309.5 .I5 2001
798.2'3--dc21
                                                          2001039987

Dedicated to the memory of Dr. Reiner Klimke
who inspired countless riders.

And to the memory of the great dressage horses
Ahlerich, Wily Trout, Keen, Gifted and Peron
who inspired all who watched them.

"Exquisite horsemanship allows the human genius to ennoble nature by design and elevate its creature, the horse, to living art."

Ethics and Passions of Dressage ~ Charles de Kunffy

Preface

As a freelance journalist in equine publishing, I've been fortunate to be able to interview riders I've always admired. But meeting them aside, what was so wonderful was they way they talked about how they achieved their own successes. In the end, each had their own story, and often times offered words of encouragement for me. It was from these experiences that the idea of this book was born.

There are many wonderful books in print to help you understand the mechanics of a shoulder-in, collection or even piaffe. This book was not written specifically as a how-to, but rather as a guide to help you move up the ladder of dressage. It is my hope that you will treat the advice given by these experts as signposts, directions to help you along your own path. Whether you desire to achieve success at Second Level or at Grand Prix, there is something for everyone here. I wish you luck and great success.

Acknowledgments

I am greatly indebted to the following people. It's such a cliché, but without them this book would truly not have been possible. First thanks to the women in my writing group: Kristen Johnston, Carol Hunter, and Elizabeth Byrd, what an incredible support system you are. Thanks also to the J-Equine Listserve, my cyber support group; my dressage trainer Jane Weatherwax and former trainers Kass Lockhart and Dianna Uphaus; Polly and Lena Dumont, Crystal Choate and Katherine Riemer who took care of my horses, Kermit and Dandy, during my "book absence." Thanks to all the dressage experts who gave their time and expertise to make this book a reality. To Moira Harris, my editor at Fancy Publications, who offered sage advice; and all the photographers who contributed their talents: Shawn Hamilton, Stacey Shaffer, Dr. Craig Chandler, Bob Langrish, Charles Mann, and Last Chance Photography. A big thank you also goes out to two wonderful guys: Tom Versen for making me laugh when I didn't want to, and to Mark Waller for the British weather reports. Last but not least, thank you to Beth Carnes, my editor at Half Halt Press, and to my family who listened to me moan about deadlines and didn't once tell me to shut up.

Contents

PART 3: COMPETING

PART 4: TIPS ON RIDING GAITS, PACES, AND MOVEMENTS

SOURCE GUIDE

PART I

The Dressage Horse

Choosing the Dressage Horse

CHRISTOPHER BARTLE

J.M. RATCLIFF

Christopher Bartle is distinguished as being one of the few riders in the world who is internationally successful in two disciplines: dressage and eventing. He was a member of the British Dressage Team from 1981 to 1987 and was the highest-ever placed British dressage rider—sixth at the 1984 Los Angeles Olympics with Wily Trout. Today, he turns his attention to eventing. Christopher is the official trainer of the British eventing team and is the managing director of the Yorkshire Riding Centre. He lives in England with his wife Susan, daughter Naomi and son Thomas.

What Makes a Dressage Horse?

Most people can do gymnastics to a level, but what makes a superstar gymnast is as much mental as it is physical—and the same applies to horses. If you're looking for a horse to go all the way to the top—to Grand Prix—and I don't mean just Grand Prix but *successful* Grand Prix at an international level, then those horses have to have a conformation that can cope with the demands of dressage, particularly with the high degree of collection.

Having said that, all horses can do dressage to a degree, but what becomes a limiting factor for the horse as you go on up the grade is partly physical—"Is nature working for them or against them?". They must have strong hindquarters and hocks with good angles at the hip, stifle and hocks. A horse that has, for example, sickle hocks, tied-in hocks or stands base narrow, is always going to struggle with the high degree of collection because these conformation problems create a strength issue, and strength is needed for collection.

The mental point of view counts as well. Very often a horse that has a very positive attitude will overcome his physical difficulties. And the horse must be tough enough and positive enough in his mental attitude to keep coming back to work. The top horses almost have to be workaholics. They have to be horses that have a natural desire to do something. They want to be energetic horses, forward-thinking horses, reactive to our aids, signals and so on. A rider is always going to be limited by a horse, who, no matter how good the conformation, has an idle nature, or from an energy point of view, is reluctant to work. A rider is always going to be held back with this sort of horse.

The Middle-Level Schoolmaster

The middle-level schoolmaster is the horse for somebody who wouldn't call himself experienced from a training or riding point of view. This rider is looking for a horse who perhaps hasn't got the range of movements to score particularly well in competition dressage but has an understanding of the movements and a willingness to perform them correctly, even if not very flamboyantly.

The middle-level schoolmaster shouldn't be too sharp in his reactions as he will be too difficult for the novice level rider to cope with. Disposition is the most important aspect for this horse to have because the middle-level rider, learning the game, has got to have a horse that tolerates the rider making the odd mistake. And he must always be willing to have a go at things. He has to be a forward-thinking horse, not one that is lazy or reluctant to perform. It's better to have a horse that is perhaps a little bit choppy in his gaits, maybe he hasn't got a fabulous medium or extended trot—but he has the capability to do good lateral work.

I find that it's easy to stereotype horses and say such and such a breed is this or that. There obviously is a tendency toward warmbloods—whether they be German, Dutch, and so on. I've come across Thoroughbreds that are lazy and I've come across warmbloods that are lazy. And I've come across very generous Thoroughbreds and very generous warmbloods. In the main, I look for a schoolmaster that fits the rider in terms of size and one that the rider can get his leg on and feel comfortable while mounted. No matter what the breed, one of the points of conformation that I think generally helps is for the horse to have a good wither and a good neck. A horse with a neck that comes out of the top of the shoulders has a natural disposition toward carrying himself in a correct dressage outline.

THE FEI SCHOOLMASTER

When a rider is looking to move on to the Fédération Equestre Internationale (FEI) levels, he should look for a horse with a good canter. The quality of the canter work—in particular the changes, canter pirouettes and canter half pass—are critical issues in the FEI tests. Generally speaking, when you're looking for dressage horses, the more important gaits are the walk and the canter. The walk and canter are what he has naturally and you aren't going to be able to change them dramatically, where his trot can be improved a lot. I look for a horse with a good canter that is capable of being connected and that doesn't have a tendency to a four-beat canter. He should have a good moment of suspension so that the changes have the potential to be correct. He also should have the ability to take the weight back on the hind legs and sit during the pirouette.

The most important thing to keep in mind when looking at the FEI schoolmaster is to look for a horse that doesn't require very strong signals for the flying changes. This is important so you can concentrate on the rhythm of the canter, on the timing of the aids, and can work on sequence changes without the horse being difficult to keep connected, keep on the bit and so forth. However, as I mentioned earlier, the horse's disposition is key to it all really. You may find a horse that tends to be a bit crooked in his changes or maybe not have the biggest changes in the world, but if he accepts the rider's aids and, no matter what, keeps thinking forward, the student will be able to learn. Having said that, one can't absolve the rider of all responsibility. No matter how good or generous a horse is, it's totally possible—and it's been seen so many times—that the rider, through confusion of the aids and the mistakes made, can end up with a horse that can't do what is asked because the rider is blocking the movement. Sometimes I've seen riders who then blame the horse and say that the horse isn't being generous, but it's really the rider blocking the movements with his reins. In car terms it's a bit like driving with one foot on the accelerator and one on the brakes at the same time.

THE MIDDLE LEVEL HORSE WITH FEI POTENTIAL

The basic requirements for a middle level horse with potential to move up to the FEI levels remains the same: good conformation, strength of the hindquarters and good strong hocks. But the back is one of the most important elements for this horse. He should have a good connection between his back and his pelvis because you don't want a horse with a natural tendency to have a hollow back and to have a weak sacroiliac

Legendary partners Rembrandt and Nicole Uphoff at the '96 Atlanta Olympics.
CLIX PHOTOGRAPHY

The middle-level schoolmaster shouldn't be too sharp in his reactions or he will be difficult for the novice rider to handle.

CLIX PHOTOGRAPHY

restricted in dressage, so look for a very round sort of action, which will help in extensions and later on in passage and piaffe work.

I wouldn't say you would want to go so far as the horse that is Hackney-like in his action. But compare that to the Thoroughbred racehorse that hardly bends his knee at all when he gallops—the flatter his stride, the more ground he can cover in a faster time. Keep in mind, you also want the rounded action in front and back. A horse that has a very round action in front, but has a tendency to elevate a very straight hind leg and not flex the angles of the hind leg when moving is a horse that would be very difficult to train.

This horse also has to have the positive attitude that we talked about earlier. He needs to be what I call a reactor: when you ask him to do something, he reacts. Even if he doesn't do the right thing, he does something. There is nothing worse than riding a horse that's got an ambition to be a statue!

area. Those sorts of things are definite no-nos for dressage. You want a strong back but not a rigid back.

Look for a horse with a definite four-beat walk, with a good swing in the back and an overtrack. In the trot, look for an easy, swinging trot, one where there is quite a degree of shoulder movement and bent forelegs. You'll sometimes see horses that float across the ground, hardly bending their knees, and not really using the shoulder very much. These types of horses are really

THE ADVANCED FEI HORSE THAT CAN COMPETE BUT NOT NECESSARILY WIN

This is a horse that has the ability to show some piaffe and passage, but maybe not brilliantly. He should have the quality of the canter and the right mental attitude to cope with the sequence flying changes and the one-time changes. This horse should be a little bit like the FEI schoolmaster we talked about earlier but with a degree beyond that.

This horse should also have a generous disposition with, again, the good conformation of the hindquarters and ability to cope with the work. This horse may not have the biggest paces in the world, which is why he won't win in top competition, but he's capable of performing all the movements consistently, say to a 60 percent level.

THE WINNING FEI HORSE

This is the sort of horse that we all dream about, that we all go mad about when we see one. This is a horse, to be perfectly honest, that you don't go out and buy. This horse comes to you. You are just lucky that you've happened to land on one. The star quality that makes a winner is something that you probably don't even realize you have until you've worked with him for awhile and developed a partnership. That horse has a confidence. Just like people, he knows he's great. He shows off, he says "Look at me." These are the stars—the ones that are going to win. You can go out to the young horse classes, you can go out looking for horses and, yes, you'll come across the one that says, "I'm your man," as it were and you'll fall in love with him. If you're lucky, that horse will go on to become a superstar, but you won't know that until you've worked with him for a couple of years.

I've had a couple of superstars in my life. One was Wily Trout. He had everything I've been talking about. He had the strength in the hindquarters, he had a real workaholic

❖ A WORD ABOUT AGE

For the schoolmaster age is not a major factor, within limits; there are always limits because dressage horses do go on. If they've gotten to age eight or nine, and they're fit and well, then they'll often go on till they're twenty-some. Again, from the schoolmaster point of view, one tolerates a degree of lack of expression and brilliance in the paces, so if the horse has the right attitude and he's happy to perform the movements, then that's what the rider of that sort of horse is looking for.

mentality; he just loved work. He maybe had too much energy in his early days, which I had to try to channel, but I never had the feeling that he wasn't giving me 110 percent. He had a great canter, but he didn't have a spectacular trot. However, that improved as we went along with our training. Because of his mental attitude he had a tremendous piaffe and passage. Wily Trout was actually a racehorse in the beginning of his career, not a flat racehorse, but bred in Ireland to become a steeplechaser. So he had a strong frame for a Thoroughbred.

I trained him to dressage because he sustained a slight tendon injury when he was eventing. That was really why we turned to dressage. We learned together. It wasn't as though I knew a lot before I started training him.

My next superstar was a Thorough-bred mare called Honey Tangle. She was a very elegant and graceful horse. She reminds me of the types of horses like Nicole Uphoff's Rembrandt and Anky van Grunsven's Bonfire.

THE TALENTED GREEN HORSE

Begin by looking at the conformation—the basic frame to hang the muscles on. Look at the leg conformation. If the horse's legs aren't straight and correct, he will run into soundness issues fairly soon. Soundness is, at the end of the day, the limiting factor, even if it's only a low-grade unsoundness. If a horse physically struggles to work, he won't want to work.

Next, look at his paces to see if he has a natural tendency to push with the hind leg and push himself onto his forehand, or whether he has a natural tendency to be, what I call, "up in front" and has a natural elevation to his paces. You're not going to know much more than that with this young horse; it's going to be very much a gut feeling. It is a gamble, but anytime you buy a horse it's a gamble. I often refer to buying horses as a bit like meeting people. You meet somebody and you have an instant liking to him or her. There is no real thought process that goes into it: You like someone or you don't. As well, it's a bit like interviewing somebody to take on a job. What you see at the interview is rarely what you get when the person starts working for you! No matter

what you may have seen or thought when you saw that young horse and bought it, you are going to have to start with a clean sheet of paper. It's your training that turns that horse into an extension of yourself.

THE YARD PROJECT: RETRAINING A HORSE WITH A PRIOR CAREER

I often get telephoned by people who say they've got a horse that they think I might be interested in for dressage because he doesn't want to jump anymore, because he's reluctant to do this, and he's reluctant to do that, and so on. And therefore they think he would be a good dressage horse. I often think that's the last sort of horse that I would want. It goes back to what we talked about earlier—the horse's disposition and character. If you're taking a horse from another discipline, whether it's from racing or hunter/jumper, his trainability is the first criteria. His natural disposition to have a good posture and to be what I would call "easy to have a dressage posture" and on the bit is the second most important thing. You don't want to start off with a horse whose nature you feel you will be working against. For example, a cutting horse who is high behind and is already built on the forehand, is going to be a no-no. You want to take a horse that's heading in the right direction in terms of his physical build to give yourself one less obstacle to overcome in his retraining.

SOUNDNESS FACTORS: WHAT IS ACCEPTABLE AND WHAT IS NOT

When it comes to soundness, you can tolerate a certain amount of problems such as, let's say, the horse isn't clean winded. They don't have to be stressed too much from that point of view for dressage since you won't be galloping cross-country. You can have a horse that has had low-grade tendon problems from perhaps his previous career. Things like bad joints—fetlocks, hocks and pasterns—are going to be the big problems. I'd be very keen to pay close examination to the joints, in particularly the hocks and the fetlocks. The horse's back is a soundness issue as well. You get horses, like people, that are predisposed to constant back trouble because they have naturally weak backs. You want a rounded loin and a good connection between the back and the pelvis through the sacroiliac.

Feet are one of my greatest concerns these days—possibly more with my eventers than with my dressage horses—but having said that, in the main, the sort of horses that we look at tend not to have bad feet. Always start out with the old Irish adage, "No hoof, no horse." You really have to start with a good foot otherwise you are in constant problems in your training with a bruised foot or heels.

There is no point doing this when evaluating a foal, but I would be inclined to X-ray the horse's joints—particularly the hocks—just to be sure that I'm not taking

Wily Trout, former point-to-pointer, proved to be Christopher Bartle's top notch dressage horse.

J.M. RATCLIFF

on a horse that has degenerative joint disease of one form or another. You're never going to find the perfect horse. And so horses that have puffy ankles, windgalls, and showing a bit of wear on his joints, if he's got to the age of 9 or 10 years old and he's still going, he's unlikely to develop conditions such as navicular. He would show signs of those by then. I would X-ray, and if he were clean, then I would be happy.

THE TRY OUT

When trying out a horse to purchase, the first thing I do is try to get comfortable on the horse and let the horse get familiar with me. I appreciate when I get on a new horse, or anyone gets on a new horse, that the horse is looking back at the rider and the rider is looking at the horse. Take a bit of time to just get to know one another. Start out with a little bit of work—walk, trot and canter. Very often I think when people go to try out a horse, they take the attitude that they are on trial themselves as riders and so they don't actually ride the horse as if it was their own. I think it's important that when you go try a horse that you take the attitude that you are actually at home training this horse. Make it go the way you think it ought to go. Try to see what his reactions are when you ask him questions. Don't back off just because you think somebody's watching you and you feel like you'd better cover up. You don't want to cover anything up; you want to find out how the horse reacts. You may do something wrong, but you want to see whether the horse tolerates you doing something wrong.

Then correct it, do it right and see whether you get a better reaction.

TIME TO MOVE ON

It's time to move on to a more advanced horse when your goals and aspirations aren't being met. Maybe you've gotten to the point where you would like some more competition success or you would like a horse that is capable of performing some of the higher-level movements. Perhaps you feel you are stuck in a rut with that particular horse. You obviously need to take some advice on that from a good trainer. Very often people stick with a horse, and in doing this, hold themselves back. I don't think a rider has to be constantly jumping from one horse to the next and getting impatient. You can always keep going with one horse and then get another horse to train alongside your schoolmaster. The change will happen naturally. As you get more obsessed with your young horse, your schoolmaster will become less important to you. Then you may find somebody else who is looking for a schoolmaster and will take him on. ▮

Horse Shopping Advice

HILDA GURNEY

Hilda Gurney is considered one of America's dressage icons. She is credited as being the person to bring dressage to the attention of American riders. In fact, many top dressage riders today credit Hilda with their successes. Riding her Thoroughbred gelding Keen she won a team bronze medal at the 1976 Olympics and also rode on the 1984 U.S. Olympic team. She raises and trains warmbloods on her ranch in Moorpark, California and competes in top-level competitions. She is a USA Equestrian "S" dressage judge.

Magazines are great sources for horses for sale.
MOIRA HARRIS

Before you start out on your shopping trip to find the perfect horse for you, think about what kind of horse you want and keep your range fairly broad. For instance, many riders don't want mares, and in saying this, they eliminate half the horse population. Or riders will say they want a specific color, and now they've narrowed the field substantially. The more you narrow things, the more difficult it will be to find the right horse, especially if you get into size, color or sex preferences. You're knocking out huge segments of the selection of horses for sale and making things very difficult for yourself.

The age of the horse is an important factor to consider, but it all depends on what you want to do with the horse. If you want a trained horse, obviously you'll need to have an older horse. If you want an untrained horse, with plans to train him yourself, you'll want to start with a fairly young horse, because if you choose an unschooled older horse, you'll run out of years to train it. So don't look for an 8-year-old to start. Once I had an owner looking for a horse—a stallion—and he had fairly unlimited funds. He found in Europe an eight-year-old "L" level (the equivalent of First Level) stallion. An eight-year-old L level is not going to have enough time, age wise, to make it to upper levels.

Another factor to consider is that a lot of horses can't do the higher level work; they just simply break down. If you are considering purchasing a 15-year-old Grand Prix horse, my guess is you'll probably get three to seven more years of work from that horse. I think the age of 23 is about the limit on a dressage horse. Once a horse has gotten to the upper level, and he's sound, meaning he can go to work drug-free, chances are, he will continue to hang it together. But the odds of a four-year-old staying sound and doing Grand Prix work are actually very slim because its difficult to tell at such an early age whether a horse will stay sound throughout the training process. I'm sure there are a high number of 4-year-olds that go lame before they get to Grand Prix because, physically, they cannot handle the stress of the work. I've been given 15-year-old horses that are sound, but don't exactly vet well, and had them still sound and working at the age of 23. They're fine because they've shown they can withstand the rigorous work.

SOURCES

Magazines are very good sources for finding horses for sale because you'll be able to find horses all around the country rather than just in your own backyard. For this same reason, there are many Web sites as well; in fact, many breed registries have Web sites that list horses for sale.

A reputable auction is another good place to look. There is a wonderful warm-blood auction on the West Coast at Glenwood Farms near Sacramento, California. The benefit to looking for a horse here is that Glenwood has been in business for a long time, has a good reputation, and they breed and select their auction horses. The Glenwood auction is very similar to the ones in Europe because the horses are pre-vetted, so you know when you get on the horse whether the results of the vet check are acceptable to you. I'm not saying the horses have passed—no horse passes or fails—but you certainly know what you're working with. At auctions, horses are generally priced quite reasonably. One or two might go for skyrocket prices, but in general you have a few high priced sellers and the rest of the horses go quite reasonably.

Many horses are for sale at shows. If you see a horse you like, ask the rider if the horse is for sale.
CRAIG CHANDLER

Another way to find good horses for sale is to contact trainers. Many of them bring in horses to sell on consignment. Steffen Peters, for instance, is constantly bringing in sale horses. Trainers advertise in magazines and at shows. Ask around to see who has sale horses in their barn.

Consider looking for a horse at the larger dressage shows; that's not always the cheapest way, but it's certainly a good way. If you see a horse at the show that you like, ask about him. Ask the person who rode the

Take time to consider what you want, search carefully, and most likely you'll find your perfect partner.

CRAIG CHANDLER

horse if he's for sale and, if not, if she or he has anything else for sale. There are a huge number of horses offered for sale at shows, and there is no better place to buy a show horse then at a horse show. A lot of the show managers help people sell horses by letting them post notices in the show office and even placing asterisks, next to the horse's name in the show program denoting that a horse is for sale.

WHAT KINDS OF QUESTIONS SHOULD A RIDER ASK?

Bottom line: if you want to buy a show horse ask about the horse's show record. That is the most important thing you need to know. I have horses at my barn that I use as schoolmasters that I will not sell because they simply don't show well. However, they are really great horses because you can learn one tempi changes, piaffe and passage. And I don't market them because I'm very ethical. For someone who isn't ethical, it would be very easy to market such a horse. But then the poor buyer would go to a show and find that the horse throws tantrums because he can't deal with the atmosphere of a horse show.

So, the show record is very important unless you are buying an unshown horse for some reason—and it had better be pretty young. If you're buying an unshown horse, ask to see the show records on the parents, because the horse's ability to cope with the show world may be hereditary.

THE PROPER WAY TO CLINCH A DEAL

Have the horse vetted first, but talk with the seller to make sure that the horse is taken off the market before you proceed with the veterinary exam. Ethically, once the horse is in vet-check status, the seller should not sell it out from under you. However, I've had horses sold from under me. The deposit system doesn't really work. I know if I receive a deposit for a horse I have for sale, and I deposit the money, if the sale doesn't go through, I have to give it back. The deposit may be $5,000, and then I have to turn around and give back the $5,000, which I have to explain to the IRS. If a seller holds the check instead of cashing it, it's really sort of worthless because the buyer can stop payment at any time. Get something in writing that says the horse is in vet check and will not be sold until the results are known.

A way to get an instant vet check is to take the horse to a large veterinary clinic. Though many sellers may not want you to haul the horse in case something happens, you may be able to hire the owner to haul him. With a very expensive horse negotiate it as one of the perks of buying him. Dicker on the price after the vet check, because no horse really passes the vet check, there is always something to consider. Think about whether you are willing or unwilling to buy the horse at the asking price from the particular results from the vet check. The vet will give you a list of what's wrong and you yourself have to decide whether you will buy the horse at that price or not. And if you want the horse for less, what percentage of the original price will you offer—and that's up to you to decide. If you aren't willing, you should get your deposit back. But buyer beware, I have known people to take my student's deposits and not give them back.

Make sure you can ride the horse. If you don't feel comfortable, don't think it's going to change.

CRAIG CHANDLER

TIPS AND PITFALLS

You need a good vet check, but the best vet check is the horse that's going out and doing his job. Be very wary of buying any horse fresh off a rest. Don't buy a horse unless he has been working consistently. The lay-up may hide a chronic problem.

You can purchase a horse that doesn't vet well at quite a reasonable price. Keep in mind that a vet check is only a guess for what the future holds; there are no guarantees. If a horse is going sound but doesn't vet well, it might not necessarily mean there will be a problem in the future.

Never get on a horse that you haven't seen ridden. There are disreputable people out there who will put you on horse that they haven't even started yet. They'll tell you the horse has been broken and it hasn't, and then you'll get a wonderful surprise and get thrown through the ground to China.

Always try the horse out as much as you can. As explained earlier, be sure he has a show record; be sure he can handle other environments besides home, be sure he's not on drugs and if he is, what kind and why? And if the horse is on medication, don't buy him, of course, things some are reasonable, preventative things such as Cosequin are okay. If you can take the horse home for a week or so to try him out and make sure he's drug free, that's ideal. But most buyers won't allow that. If the horse is on tranquilizers of any sort, don't buy him. No matter how much you think the horse couldn't change that much, he will. And have a drug test done. I know drug tests are very expensive, but they are well worth it rather than being stuck with a worthless horse.

Be sure you buy a horse with an uphill type of conformation. Lots of people buy these huge movers that are actually built on the forehand. You do want a good mover, but you don't need a huge mover. However, make sure the horse has extensions. It's interesting to note that some of the really huge movers don't have extensions. The horse's working trot is huge, but you ask for the next button and nothing's there.

Make sure you can ride the horse. If you don't feel comfortable on him, don't think anything is going to change. If you get on the horse and you feel like you click with that horse, buy him. But if you get on him and you say, "Oh, I don't click with the horse but I'll grow into him," don't buy him. Don't let somebody tell you that you'll learn how to ride the horse, because you won't. In the same vein, don't buy a horse you can't sit, put on the bit, one that scares you or one that doesn't respond to your aids.

Don't buy a horse until you try it at least three times on different days. Make sure the horse hasn't worked hard before you ride him or that the seller hasn't withheld water from him. Disreputable people will do these kinds of things. Look in the horse's stall to make sure he has water. Look for little tricks, like the seller hiding a horse's mouth problem by giving him a piece of apple. The horse tries to suck the apple off the bit and he keeps his tongue in the entire time you ride him. Then after you buy him, you've found that the horse keeps his tongue out, and you've now got a useless horse.

You can look for stable vices by looking at the condition of the horse's stall. See if he's been kicking the walls. Watch the horse in the cross ties and on the ground. Groom him and saddle him yourself.

Take the time to consider what you want, search carefully and wisely and most likely you'll find a good horse at the price you can afford. ▌

Horse Shopping in Europe

MERRIE VELDEN

STACEY SHAFFER

Merrie Velden started out riding Icelandic ponies as a child in her home state of Wisconsin. She received her formal riding education at 17 at Meredith Manor on West Virginia. It was there that she got her first taste of dressage. It wasn't until after taking up several jobs training horses of all disciplines that she actually settled on dressage as a sport in 1987. She rode as a member of the United States Equestrian Team from 1994–1998. She makes several trips to Europe each year to find horses for her clients. She is based in San Diego, California.

Shopping for a horse can be really exciting. Buying your new partner is like opening another chapter in your competition or learning career. On the other hand, locating the right horse can be frustrating sometimes: you'll make tons of phone calls, travel across the country to follow up on a lead that may take you nowhere, and pay lots of money for vet checks. Many times all that traveling and frustration can result in having no horse at all. Think about expanding your search by traveling to Europe.

There are several pluses to taking your search overseas: In Europe horses are bred and raised by lots of people. Just like America is the land for Quarter Horses, Europe is the land for sporthorses. After all, Europeans are the ones that initially bred the warmblood for sport. The second plus is, depending on the exchange rate, you can find well-trained horses at better prices in Europe. Third, most barns have several horses that you can check out, whereas, here in America you may be traveling from barn to barn looking at one horse at a time. (Consider the fact that you can drive across Germany in one day.) Many countries in Europe, such as Germany, are farming countries and horses are commodities. In America it can be very difficult to find a good horse with good training at a reasonable price. In Germany, you can go to the biggest pig farm you've ever seen and buy fabulous dressage horses. One of the best young horses I've ever seen was at the piggiest pig farm. I mean it stunk so bad, and there was this black/bay horse that seem to have the word "Olympic" tattooed on its butt—and he didn't cost very much money. If it's a competitive schoolmaster you're after, Europe is definitely the place to look. In Germany if a horse is doing Prix St. Georges at 12 years old they think the horse isn't going anywhere and the value drops severely. You can pick up a sound schoolmaster very reasonably.

FIRST THINGS FIRST

The first thing you need to do is to get in touch with an agent in Europe. It helps if you have somebody who speaks the language and has an understanding of the area, the horses and the people who have trained them. An agent will fill this bill. You also need a connection to a good vet—one who knows what problems you will and will not accept. You have to be very sure that this horse vets well because you're spending a lot of money to bring him back to the United States—around $5,000.

How do you find such people? There are many trainers in jumping, eventing, and dressage in the United States who know people in Europe who can help you. All the big-name trainers have been to Europe, and many of them are happy to help. Understand that if you're given a name of a well-known agent, you'll need to remember the trainer when a deal is made. These trainers have worked for years to make good connections, and they deserve a commission from your purchase. Ask the trainer how they would like their commission to be handled in the event of a sale. Some trainers get the fee from the overseas agent, while some prefer to receive the money directly from you. Agents usually work on a commission basis as well, but you'll want to discuss the fee before you leave.

Many trainers recommend that you go to a famous trainer's facility such as Karin Rehbein's or Johann Hinnemann's. If this is the case, expect to pay a lot of money. These people are big-name dealers, and they specialize in selling dressage horses to Americans. The average price of a First Level horse at a barn like this is around $50,000. If this isn't your budget, ask your trainer for the name of an agent who does business with smaller brokers who deal in quantity. Agents also deal with amateur riders who are selling their own horses, but don't think that the training will be less than perfect. You have to understand that many amateurs in Germany can out-ride our trainers. When I say, "Go talk to Viola. She has a friend who has a friend, who wants to sell her Fourth Level horse," rest assured that horse is a solid Fourth Level horse. But these are the realistic people who are not making a killing on the horses like the big guys.

Your agent will have selected several barns to visit before you arrive. Once you arrive he will take you to the barns and speak to the farmer or trainer for you. Bring along a knowledgeable trainer or horseperson as well—someone who can make sure this is a good horse for you. If you are undertaking a purchase by yourself, ask the owner to let you see the horse rid-

❖ THE LIST OF CONS

1. When shopping for a horse in Europe, you can't always find the history of the horse. At a sales barn, a horse can come in from Holland, Sweden, Denmark and even Russia. You don't know who last had that horse, when its last shots were or how it was trained etc. This may not be a big issue for some people, but keep this in mind as you ask your questions.

2. You may have to wade through lots of not-so-good horses. But unlike in America, they keep dragging lots of horses out of stalls. You've got many choices, a lot of farms within a smaller area and plenty of fabulous horses and barns you wouldn't even believe exist.

3. Shopping in Europe still can be expensive, especially if you don't do it right. You have to know horses, and you have to be able to evaluate a horse very well. If you set up a vet check, you want to be there to make sure your needs are being met.

den outside in a field, in a snaffle, particularly if he's an FEI horse. You don't want a horse that needs to be ridden exclusively in a double bridle. Ask if you can watch him tack the horse etc. One thing you have to remember is that Europeans do things differently than Americans. They don't clip their horses much, and a lot of their horses don't like spray bottles or having water hosed onto them. In general, Europeans don't believe in washing horses much, clipping, or spraying them with fly spray. They have a different way of horsemanship, and they spend a lot more time grooming horses instead of bathing and clipping. So expect your horse to react differently to your way of doing things.

Is it easier to shop in Europe? Well, maybe not, but you may be able to get a nifty well-trained horse that's sound and gorgeous. And think of the great adventure that waits for you—certainly the shopping trip of a lifetime. ▌

Bringing Your European Horse Home

SHARON BIGGS

SHARON FIBELKERK

*Award-winning writer Sharon Biggs has written for many magazines including **Dressage & CT, Dressage Today, Horse Illustrated, Chronicle of the Horse, Equine Athlete,** and **Horses USA,** and in the United Kingdom, **Horse Magazine**. She is a former dressage trainer and riding instructor, and has served as chairman of the San Diego Chapter of the California Dressage Society. She is awaiting the publication of her first children's book. Sharon divides her time between Kent, England and San Diego, California.*

Etienne, one of Christine Traurig's successful imports.

CLIX PHOTOGRAPHY

You've searched high and low. You've found the perfect horse, and he's passed the vet check. What's next? The agent will help you negotiate a price and will organize the shipment of your new baby. He'll arrange with a company to haul your horse to the airport located in Amsterdam, Frankfurt or Luxembourg City. The airlines that import horses are KLM (a Dutch airline and the main carrier of horses), Lufthansa (a close second but not used as much), Cargo Lux (an airline working out of Luxembourg), and now FedEx is getting into the game.

You will have to select the city nearest you with quarantine facilities as your destination. Your airliner will let you know which airport has them.

You'll need an agent on the US end because it is difficult to handle the shipping on your own, so your next step is to contact an animal freight forwarder. Your European agent can recommend someone and but most of the time these agents operate out of airport quarantine facilities. The animal freight forwarder can help you by providing lots of services such as handling red tape. You will be required to test your horse in Europe for four diseases: dourine, glanders (a disease contagious to humans), equine infections anemia (a coggins test) and piroplasmosis. If your new horse tests positive to any of these diseases he will not be permitted to leave. If he tests positive in America while under quarantine he will not be permitted to stay. Both your European and US agent (animal freight forwarder) will help you organize this.

Your US agent will also find two other horses to share the jet container with your horse. Each container is capable of holding one to three horses. If you choose to have your horse share the container with one horse or none, realize that you're going to spend more money. How much? The price fluctuates because the airline charges the price in the foreign currency. However, expect to pay $10,000 for the entire container plus government fees and health certificates. Make sure you add this price into your shopping budget.

Note: Mares and stallions are different than geldings or very young horses because they are tested for CEM—contagious equine metritis—a venereal disease. After this quarantine they move to another facility where they are tested for CEM. Mares stay for an additional two weeks and stallions stay longer. If a mare or a stallion is in your future, budget in more money and time.

The quarantine facility is required to do blood work and to make sure the horse is healthy and can be released into the general horse population. Quarantine usually lasts about 48 hours—basically the amount of time it takes to process the horses and ship the blood to Ames, Iowa, to be tested. Sometimes horses get stuck in quarantine due to the blood test results being held up.

The horses are typically flown in a combi-jet: a plane that carriers people in one half and cargo in the other. KLM provides grooms that are actually crew members trained on the operations of the aircraft. The boxes are fully enclosed—just like being in a horse trailer. They usually travel well, however, horses are the most difficult commodity to ship, so you have very little room for error. The industry has done a great job in limiting risks—designing good shipping boxes, and offering more jet stalls, enclosed boxes, professional grooms, and handling the horses quickly. The horses usually are in the quarantine barn within an hour of their arrival. The horses go through customs procedures in the air, but the grooms must pass through customs on the airplane before they travel off the plane with the horses.

The best dressage horses are not necessarily found in top trainer's barns. Former police horse, Goldstern, proved his mettle in the dressage arena time and time again.

CHARLES MANN

The USDA (U.S. Department of Agriculture) vet follows the horses off the jet and to the quarantine facility where he oversees the processing of the horses. The horses remain in the container until they arrive at quarantine. Then the containers are loaded onto a flatbed pickup truck. The truck backs up to the facility and everyone involved puts on overalls and boots that can be disinfected after the horses are cared for.

The horses are then off-loaded onto a ramp and into the quarantine yard. The horses arrive with identification tags in their manes, but the vets also put a sticker onto their rumps with their names on it for easier identification. An insecticide is swabbed into their nose and ears to kill lurking insects, then they are sprayed down with the same insecticide. They are taken into their stalls where they are offered a bran mash and some timothy hay. Blood is drawn and sent off to the laboratory.

If you're lucky enough to live near a quarantine facility, you can come see your horse arriving. Although you can't touch your horse, you may be able to stand behind a fence to watch. If you can't, rest assured he will be taken care of. Your agent will see your horse onto a trailer to be shipped to you. ∎

The Prepurchase Exam

DR. A. KENT ALLEN, D.V.M.

BRANT GAMMA PHOTOGRAPHY

Dr. Kent Allen is a 1979 graduate of the University of Missouri College of Veterinary Medicine. Today, he's located in Middleburg, Virginia in an equine practice that specializes in lameness, prepurchase exams, and state-of-the-art diagnostic imaging. He is chairman of both the USA Equestrian Veterinary Committee and their Drug and Medication Committee. He serves as the North American representative on the veterinary committee for the Fédération Equestre Internationale. He has also served as a United States Equestrian Team veterinarian at international competitions around the world including the Olympics ('96 and 2000). Dr. Allen was one of the early adopters of equine ultrasonography and became one of the first practitioners to introduce nuclear scintigraphy and thermography into veterinary practice.

Most veterinarians involved with the sport of dressage who are participating in a prepurchase examination have a similar goal: to assist the rider in the physical examination of a horse they have deemed suitable for the task intended. Therefore, the goal is to help the rider find the correct horse—not to fail a horse.

Before we launch into the specifics of the examination, I would like you to keep the following in mind:

• No horse is perfect. All horses have some imperfections that will be major or minor in magnitude depending on what the horse is selected to do in its career.

• The veterinarian should enter the examination without concern for legal liability. His or her focus should be on a thorough exam to determine if the horse is suitable for intended usage.

• The buyer should understand there is no such thing as a crystal ball. The veterinarian is looking at the horse at a specific point in time with the history he is given. He cannot predict how a particular animal will perform in the future. The veterinarian performing the prepurchase exam is not the buyer's insurance policy for the horse staying sound. If the buyer wants that he should purchase a loss-of-use insurance policy and be sure that the insurance company will issue a policy on the horse in question.

• It is always easier to evaluate a horse that is doing the job that it is intended to do than it is to look at a youngster with no experience and speculate on what the horse might be able to do in the future.

WHO IS INVOLVED IN THE PREPURCHASE EXAM?

The Buyer: The buyer has the most worrisome role as it is his money that will purchase the horse he hopes will compete successfully at the intended level. To help in the decision, the buyer assembles a supporting cast of advisors. At no time, however, can the buyer abdicate any of the ultimate responsibility for the purchase of the horse.

The Seller: The seller has a traumatic role to play. He is selling a horse in which he has invested years of training, or he has a young prospect for which he has high hopes. No seller likes to be told there is anything wrong with his horse. The prepurchase exam is designed to find out any possible problems with the horse and then assign significance to them according to the horse's intended purpose.

The Agent: The agent has expertise in selecting a horse for the buyer when the buyer is unable to find one himself. He often has multiple connections within the horse market and/or multiple young horses that he is bringing along for sale himself. The agent, having found the horse, has a vested interest in seeing the sale completed. He or she often earns a percentage for his or her connections and ability to find horses for a given task.

The Trainer: The trainer has an interest in helping the buyer procure the horse as he will train the horse and rider to develop a successful combination. Often a trainer is very involved in the acquisition and purchase of a new horse or replacement horse for a dressage rider. He can offer a wealth of expertise concerning a horse's suitability to reach the competition goals as set by the buyer.

The Veterinarian: The veterinarian is the medical advisor. His or her opinion is sought to make sure the horse does not have confirmation, physical or lameness problems that will limit its ability to perform at a given level. It is very important to all parties involved at which the veterinarian have significant experience with the level of competition at which the buyer is expecting the horse to perform. The reason that this is so important is that at the end of the exam the veterinarian will need to put the imperfections or problems that he has found into perspective with what the horse will be asked to do. This part of the exam is critical and very difficult to achieve if the veterinarian does not have significant experience with this type of horse. The veterinarian will not pass or fail the horse since each prepurchase exam varies depending on what the buyer is expecting of that particular horse.

THE BASIC EXAMINATION

The basic examination has many individual variations, even among veterinarians within the same practice. The prepurchase examination calls on the detective and intuitive skills of the veterinarian to find any lameness and medical problems. He then incorporates his experience to explain what

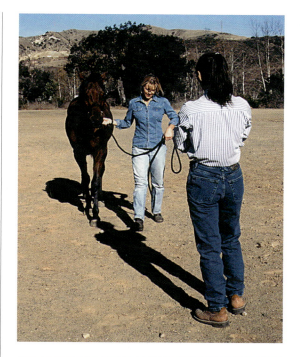

The vet's job is to help assist the rider to determine if their future is up for the task of dressage.

LAST CHANCE PHOTOGRAPHY

those problems mean in light of the intended use of the horse. This is easily the most complex examination that veterinarians are called on to perform. The lameness examination, on the other hand (which is different from the prepurchase exam), is simple because it has a stated goal—to determine if a horse has a lameness problem that is causing substandard performance.

In the prepurchase exam, the horse is examined by systems (heart, lungs, etc.) or by anatomic regions (right front limb, etc.). The most common method is to begin by taking a brief history of any illnesses or lameness problems the horse may have had. Obviously, recent problems are of greater concern. Usually I ask what the horse has been doing for the past three to six months. The answer will determine if the horse has been at work or at rest. If the horse has been at rest, I want to know why. If the exam is taking place near the horse's stall, I look in it for evidence of cribbing or other stall vices. These vices are rarely a medical problem but often are of concern to a buyer. The general attitude of the horse and the basic conformation usually is examined at this time. The horse's markings are noted on a worksheet so if there is a question at a later date it can be proven which horse was examined on that day.

The Head: The head is often examined first, beginning with a thorough opthalmic examination of the eyes. The sinuses are lightly tapped to make sure they have a normal resonant sound and are not filled with scar tissue or evidence of old infection. The ears are looked at to see if there is any evidence of viral growths, or tumors or discharge. The mouth is examined to see if the given age corresponds to the approximate dental aging, and any identification tattoo is recorded. I look to see if the teeth align properly and if there is need for dental care. A brief neurological examination is performed on the head to make sure the cranial nerves appear to be within normal limits.

The Respiratory System: The respiratory system is examined by auscultation (listening with a stethoscope). I listen to the trachea and lung areas, and the horse is usually encouraged to take a few deep breaths. This is accomplished either by holding the nose for a brief period of time or by using a plastic bag, or it may be done after the horse is exercised. Respiratory rates are taken during rest and after exercise. Any respiratory noise during exercise is noted.

The Cardiovascular System: The cardiovascular system consists of the heart and corresponding arteries and veins within the body. The heart is listened to for a normal rhythm and an absence of a murmur. Filling of the jugular veins and the leg veins, particularly in the hind legs, is evaluated after exercise. Any filling of the hind legs on a normal basis is also noted. The heart rate is taken while the horse is resting, and again after exercise.

The Gastrointestinal System: The gastrointestinal system is evaluated as to whether the horse looks thrifty and is in good flesh. The intestinal sounds are monitored for any abnormalities, and in the southern states, for evidence of sand heard in the lower portion of the intestine. The lower abdomen is observed for any evidence of past colic surgery.

The Musculoskeletal System: The musculoskeletal system is one of the key points in the examination of a dressage horse. This system must have the conformation necessary to support the horse in the work that it has been chosen to do. Fairly major conformational flaws may be present in a lower-level horse but the horse still may be able to do its job. Upper-level horses, however, will tolerate only fairly minor conformational flaws because these flaws will rapidly affect performance as the horse continues to accumulate experience in the upper levels as well as wear and tear.

Usually I first look over the horse to determine if surgery has been performed to enhance the musculoskeletal system. I check the stifle area where a medial patellar desmotomy, a surgical procedure in which joint stability is improved by cutting the medial patellar ligament, may have been performed. I look for scars in the heel area which would indicate a neurectomy (best known as "nerving" where a surgical procedure is done to block pain. This is often used to manage navicular disease.) had been performed. Simply testing the heels for sensation is not an accurate enough test, since horses that have had neurectomies regain surface sensation, but not deep pain, within a matter of weeks.

The horse's back is examined in detail and palpated for muscle soreness in the back and croup area. Next, the dorsal spine is palpated from the withers back to the sacroiliac area. These areas are examined for pain on palpation. Some pain on muscular palpation is not uncommon for horses in competition.

Shoeing is also evaluated at this point with the horse being examined on a flat, level surface. The horse is then moved in hand at a walk and trot, and I look to see whether the feet land flat and level. The feet are then examined to see if they are the same size. Unusual foot conformation, such as high heel, or low heel front foot conformation is noted as this may cause problems later.

The hoof is examined for signs of lameness.
CLIX PHOTOGRAPHY

This also is the time that I stand back from the horse and look for lumps and bumps, swelling in the fetlock or other points in the legs. Wind puffs or tendon sheath filling can become a problem, particularly if located low in the back of the hind fetlock area. Mild to moderate filling in tendon sheaths is a common finding in the dressage horse and is not of major concern unless it is associated with heat or pain on palpation or flexion of the limb. Particularly, I pay attention to the suspensory ligament branches, since these are commonly injured in dressage horses.

The prepurchase exam calls on the detective and intuitive skills of the veterinarian.

LAST CHANCE PHOTOGRAPHY

Next, each leg is evaluated in turn for pain by hoof-tester response. It is preferable that the horse has not been shod within the prior week as occasionally there will be little sole present and false positive readings may result. The leg is then palpated for any pain or thickening in the tendons and ligaments. Pain on palpation is a highly subjective finding, and I attempt to correlate it with thickening before making a clinical judgment. Occasionally a horse

will be subjected to additional tests such as diagnostic ultrasound to determine whether the horse simply flinches when it is palpated or if there is a real problem. The joints are flexed for evidence of full range of motion. This is what is called "passive flexion" since the horse is not jogged afterwards. I am checking to see that the horse bends his legs easily and it has a normal range of movement.

The horse is examined at a walk and trot on a straight, flat surface. He is then moved on a longe line and/or under saddle at a walk, trot and canter, usually on firm footing that has a good surface. I look for any indication of lameness as evidenced by a head bob or a body drop from one side to another. If I have any questions after seeing the horse on the longe line or if the horse has significant back soreness, I would definitely want to see the horse under saddle.

The next part of the exam is the "active flexion" test, which is flexion of the joints or limbs followed by jogging. This exam is simply a flexion test of the joint and then the horse is jogged away. It is acceptable for the horse to move stiffly or lame for a few steps after the flexion. The question is whether the horse is comparable side to side, and whether the horse takes an extended time to warm out of the flexion. Obviously horses with older arthritic joints or horses that have been in recent competition will take longer to warm out of the flexion tests. This is usually equal from side to side, unless the problem is worse on one side than the other. This exam simply compares the horse to itself, not to other horses. It should never be used as a basis to eliminate a horse from consideration. It is simply used as an indicator of a potential problem that may need to be X-rayed or further evaluated.

The Neurological Evaluation: A neurological evaluation is usually performed during the physical and the musculoskeletal examinations. If a question is raised as to the ability of the horse to move its limbs normally, additional tests are performed. Some of these tests may include moving the horse in tight circles, and others may be blood or spinal-tap tests for equine protozoal myelitis (EPM). I normally do not take blood tests routinely for EPM unless the horses show some neurological signs, since 50 percent of normal horses in the United States will have a positive blood test to EPM

Blood Work: The coggins test, which is required by most states for interstate transportation, is also recommended as a routine part of the prepurchase exam by the American Association of Equine Practitioners (AAEP). This is a test for equine infectious anemia. Although it is rare to find a positive reactor, a horse that does test positive will be quarantined by federal authorities for the rest of its life.

If the horse is being imported from a foreign country, then blood tests for diseases that would keep the horse from entering the United States or from going abroad to compete, should be checked before money changes hands.

OPTIONAL TESTS:

X-rays: X-rays (radiographs) are routinely taken as part of the prepurchase exam. Any set of X-rays will inevitably have false positives, which are X-ray changes not significant to the lameness or to the intended use of the horse. The X-rays are the best possible guide to describing any hint of future problems such as low-level arthritis or bone cystic disease that, although present, will not cause a problem until later when a horse is in heavier work.

Realistically, X-rays may value or devalue a horse in today's market. The rule of thumb is if you do not like the X-rays today, you will like them even less in three years when you go to sell the horse. Also, if there is a previous set of X-rays existing on a horse, they often can be used to argue that navicular changes in the front feet have been unchanged for the past three years. A complete set of prepurchase radiographs also gives you valuable information by which to base: (1) the purchase decision, (2) a baseline for that particular horse and (3) a basis for later arguing that insignificant X-ray changes in the horse have been unchanged over a period of time.

A common set of X-rays done for the prepurchase of a dressage horse would be a front-to-back view of the navicular bone, a lateral view of the navicular and foot and a flexor view of the navicular in both front feet. Front-to-back and side views of all four fetlocks are also quite common. Because of the propensity for hock problems in any horse utilizing its hind legs, as the dressage horse must, it is also common to have a full series consisting of front to back, side and two oblique views of each hock. If there is filling in any of the fetlock joints, additional radiographs may be required. If it is a young horse (particularly young warm-bloods) stifle radiographs may be neccessary to rule out any bone disease.

If the horse has a prepurchase exam performed outside the U.S. or out of town, it is advisable to have the X-ray records examined by your veterinarian or by a veterinarian familiar with the level of dressage horse you are buying. These veterinarians should be able to give you insights on whether the radiographs are within normal limits and the significance of any changes.

Scoping: A scoping or endoscopic exam is done for dressage horses only if respiratory noise is heard in exercise.

Drug Testing: Drug testing is an option for the buyer if he is in a situation where he feels uncomfortable or unsure. Drug testing ensures that the horse has no medication in its bloodstream that would significantly affect the horse at the time of the examination.

Bone Scan: The bone scan is a technique used to look at the active inflammation or physiology of the bone itself. This is totally different from an X-ray which looks only at the anatomical changes within the bone. The bone scan can be used to help focus on whether an X-ray change is significant to a particular horse. It can also be used to give a wide overview of any inflammatory changes in the horse. It also can be used to answer questions that have been raised in the X-rays.

Thermography: This is surface temperature mapping of the horse. Thermography is a rapid method of evaluating surface inflammatory changes in the horse and is useful for looking at specific areas or a wide overview of the horse. This can be used as a screening test.

Fluoroscopy: Fluoroscopy, or Xiscan, is a moving or real time X-ray examination. The machine is portable and is usually faster than standard X-rays. As in any set of diagnostics there are trade-offs. For the ease, quickness and portability, you usually wind up with a lower resolution X-ray than with standard flat films. I recommend that standard flat films are made for the permanent record.

Video Examination: Buyers who are interested in a horse located far away often use videotapes to let their veterinarian or trainer see the horse. Videos can be useful in critical evaluation if they are done properly. The horse should be walked and trotted away from the camera, then walked and trotted toward the camera on a hard, level surface. The horse should then be walked and trotted with the camera out to the side of the horse. This should be done at least twice in each direction. Next, the horse should be taken into an arena and trotted on a lunge line or ridden with a loose rein in both directions and cantered in both directions. The entire length of the video should be no longer than five to 10 minutes.

It is useful to see the horse at work or a video of the horse working. Particularly, it is helpful to see the horse performing extensions and trot work as well as lateral work.

Ultrasound: Ultrasound, or sonography, is the use of sound waves to study the body—-particularly soft tissue. Ultrasound should be used anytime there is a thickening and/or pain response on tendon palpation. It is particularly useful in determining if a horse's rehabilitated or healed tendon or ligament will hold up to additional stresses such as moving up a level.

Lameness Examination: If a buyer and seller so desire, the prepurchase exam can change into a lameness exam. This might occur if, for example, a horse is noticed to be lame during the prepurchase exam. Usually this involves a discussion with both the buyer and seller to see if everyone agrees to blocking the leg with a local anesthetic to determine the exact area where the horse is lame. If so, is it in a location that is considered to be of minor consequence or one that can be treated easily? One of the optional or diagnostic tests would be performed on that area to determine what the problem is and how it would affect the future of the horse. Obviously, by definition, a horse cannot be considered suitable for the usage intended if it is lame at the time of exam. It is not uncommon to work out an arrangement whereby the horse may be re-examined at a later date once the determination of the problem has been made.

The prepurchase exam is extremely useful for gathering information on which to base a purchase decision. It should be re-emphasized that the buyer has the ultimate authority and responsibility, and the veterinarian, trainer, agent, etc., are advisors who can offer experience and probabilities of what may happen, but they cannot predict the future of that individual horse. In the end, the buyer must decide, in light of all the information he has been given, if he wants "a horse" or he wants "this horse." ▌

Feeding the Dressage Horse

DR. PAUL McCLELLAN, D.V.M.

STACEY SHAFFER

Dr. Paul McClellan is a graduate of Purdue University School of Veterinary Medicine. Since 1982, he has practiced in northern San Diego County, devoting his efforts exclusively to performance horses. He has worked with horses competing in dressage, eventing, racing and jumping. He is a Federation Equestre Internationale veterinary delegate for the United States and has published numerous articles relating to the use of diagnostic ultrasound imaging for the horse. He advises top riders on what feeds are best for hard-working sporthorses.

Feeding the horse is a subject of great mystery and confusion, particularly when complex equations and scientific terms are tossed about in an effort to persuade the consumer that one product is superior to another. In this chapter I will limit my comments on numbers, equations and scientifically laced terminology to the bare minimum necessary for a practical understanding of nutrition. I will deal with the topics, which are the most frequent source of confusion, and those problems most often encountered during the course of my clinical rounds.

There are a few terms you should understand:

Roughage: These are all the hays, such as alfalfa, timothy, etc. They are high in non-digestible fiber and may be fed as loose hay, or in cubed, chopped or pelleted forms. Roughage is ultimately the source of approximately 90 percent of the nutrients that a horse needs simply because it is the single largest component (by weight) of what a horse eats. Because of the anatomy of the horse's digestive tract, large amounts of high-fiber feed are necessary. You simply cannot supply adequate nutrition without good quality roughage. Conversely, poor quality hay is the source of many problems found in managed horses. Problems such as hives, diarrhea, colic, respiratory allergies, and poor muscling and weight are frequently traced back to poor quality hay. Simply put, it pays to feed good quality roughage.

Concentrates: This category includes all of the different grains that a horse may eat—barley, soy bean, oats (oat hay is a roughage not a concentrate), corn, wheat, bran, etc. These are called concentrates because they contain usable energy that is primarily in the form of carbohydrates without the bulk (fiber) of hay.

Supplements: These are all of the other items that you may choose to add to the feed bucket—such things as vitamins, electrolytes, etc. Oil and fat-based products are a special case. Originally they were added to feed in small amounts in order to supply essential fat-soluble vitamins and other essential fatty acids that are necessary for health and for a shiny hair coat (especially when horses are getting bathed frequently). It has now been recognized that horses can easily accept larger amounts of fat in their diet as a source of "concentrated" energy. The energy value of fat is more than double that of an equal (by weight) amount of grain. That is a main reason why we see so many high-fat feeds on the market (such as the rice-bran products). Technically fat is a concentrate, not a supplement, and it has proved very useful to provide necessary calories (energy) for hard-working horses.

Water: Water is the single most important nutrient for a horse. It may seem an obvious point that water is necessary for health, yet it is so often overlooked when assessing the quality of the diet. Horses have preferences about water taste and temperature. It most often becomes a critical factor with travel and with extremes of temperature. When traveling, I often recommend feeding a wet bran mash when the horse arrives at its destination to stimulate the

Even if you board your horse, know what and how your horse eats.

appetite and help the horse recover from the dehydration of travel. Another method is to use an oral electrolyte paste, which is commonly sold over the counter. This seems to stimulate water consumption when given after travel or strenuous exercise. Finally, if in doubt about the hydration status of your horse call a veterinarian and ask if a treatment with intravenous fluids is appropriate. It is one of the quickest methods to get a tired horse back on track.

Studies have shown that horses drink less when the temperature of the water is too hot or too cold. Be attentive to the temperature and amount of water your horse consumes daily and during travel.

In large, private stables, quite often the responsibility of feeding falls to the grooms or barn manager. It is not unusual for the owner or trainer not to know what the horse is being fed and, just as important, how well the horse is eating. Only if the horse has a problem with colic, weight loss or performance is the subject reviewed in any detail. In public stables, all horses are fed a basic amount of roughage because individualizing feeding is not effective from the stable owners point of view. Those doing the feeding are not responsible for evaluating the horse's appetite, performance or behavior. In small, private stables, feeding receives the most individualized attention, but errors still occur due to lack of knowledge or misinformation. Consequently, my first guideline of feeding is, know what and how your horse eats and drinks.

If one were to survey the diets of the top equine competitors in any equestrian discipline, it would be apparent that there is a significant variability in the type of roughage, the amount of concentrate and the number of supplements that are being fed to any particular animal. Add to this the fact that variability exists due to other external and internal factors such as feed quality, feed availability, environment, age of the animal, intensity of work and each horse's individual rate of metabolism. It quickly becomes overwhelming then for someone who wishes to develop a diet that will maximize performance and not be harmful or wasteful to the horse. This variability is the reason hard numbers for feeding are difficult to come by. The one great factor in our favor is that horses, like most other warm-blooded mammals, have a great ability to adapt to a variety of diets, extracting from feed the necessary nutrients to maintain a healthy body. Just exactly how this occurs is a subject of ongoing research, but for our purposes it works in our favor. Why then should we worry at all? The answer is what I call the one percent rule. For the healthy mature performance horse, providing the best diet improves performance one percent over an adequate diet, and in competition one percent means the difference between winners and losers. For the noncompetitive horse, that one percent may be the difference between a healthy, sound horse of longevity and a horse that borders on chronic lameness, colic, allergies, or immune incompetence.

The second guideline of feeding is that it is a dynamic—or constantly changing—process. All of the factors we discussed earlier, and others, predicate the necessity of regular review and modification of a horse's feeding program. One of the primary factors is simply based on how much work the horse is receiving. A young horse in beginning training or a mature horse in light training will need primarily roughage. Do not ever settle for moldy, dusty hay. Feed the best quality hay you can find because as stated earlier, 90 percent of the nutrient value of the diet is in the hay. I personally recommend a small amount of concentrate even for horses in light work. A concentrate with an added vitamin/mineral supplement rounds out the diet insuring that the need for trace minerals and other micronutrients are met.

As it proceeds to full work, a horse may need as much as 12–6 quarts of concentrate per day or roughly 40–50 percent of the total energy (not weight) of the diet

Roughage is the source of 90 % of your horse's nutrients.

LAST CHANCE PHOTOGRAPHY

from grain. This is because exercising horses may not be able to move enough roughage through their system fast enough to gain enough energy for the amount of work being done. Remember, concentrates have roughly 20–30 percent more digestible energy per unit weight than roughage. There are several potential problems when feeding high amounts of grain to horses. Behavioral changes, gastrointestinal upset and excess heat production are possible manifestations of excess grain in the diet. There is a difference in the way carbohydrates in grains are metabolized as compared to fat. If your horse has difficulty keeping a good energy level or good weight under hard work, discuss with your veterinarian the use of fat to replace some of the grain. As stated before, fats are an even more concentrated source of energy than either hay or grains. I recommend some fat for all working horses unless

Concentrates contain usable energy in the form of carbohydrates.

CLIX PHOTOGRAPHY

the individual has difficulty keeping weight off. For hard working dressage horses, feeding dietary fat may provide a significant portion of the energy necessary to maintain proper weight. Fat is also a good source of vitamins A, D and E, and essential fatty acids. Care must be taken during production and when stored at the barn not to let it go rancid, thereby losing its beneficial contents.

As the horse approaches the time of competition, another adjustment often is necessary to the diet depending on whether the horse works harder or less hard in the few weeks before the show. Those that lose weight due to nervousness, anorexia or hyperactivity all may have different nutritional needs. The nervous horse may benefit from more time out of the stall and more frequent opportunities to eat. The anorexic horse may have an "acid stomach" and benefit from antacid or ulcer medications. The hyperexcitable horse may need less grain and increased fat in the diet. In some warmbloods a defect has been identified in the normal storage of carbohydrates in the muscles leading those horses to exhibit myositis or tie-up syndrome. Increasing the amount of fat as an energy source and reducing the carbohydrate (grains) has been advocated for this situation. Discuss this with your veterinarian before changing the diet for this purpose.

FEEDING DURING INJURY OR DISEASE

One of the areas where nutritional balance is commonly neglected is when a horse must have his training discontinued due to an injury or illness. When the horse goes on the turnout list for several months, the feed is often reduced drastically so the horse does not run around too much and aggravate the injury. It is my opinion that, although this time of reduced energy intake is necessary to keep a horse from getting fat or "wild," it is still imperative to provide vitamins, minerals and properly balanced nutrients, all of which are necessary for the healing processes. A horse healing a fracture may need calcium/phosphorus supplementation. A horse recovering from shipping fever or pneumonia may need more energy than he is willingly eating. Horses receiving medication for EPM (Equine Protozoal Myeloencephalitis) may need folic acid supplementation. A horse recovering from colic surgery has high metabolic demands to regain lost weight and re-establish normal intestinal function. Young, growing horses and those just returning from a lay up need good quality protein when the demand to build muscle is at its greatest. This time of relative inactivity then should not be neglected from a nutritional standpoint.

SUPPLEMENTATION OF THE DIET

There are great philosophical arguments about supplements. It is my belief that the majority of horses in athletic training would benefit from some supplementation in their diets. As an example, would the horse that fails to develop good muscle of the neck, shoulders or hindquarters benefit from a muscle-building supplement? What about a horse that seems prone to respiratory or skin infections: Would using an oral immune stimulant be beneficial if a bonafide one existed? Does the heavy-sweating horse need extra electrolytes? What supplement will breathe fire into the lazy horse, calm the excited one, or trim fat from the chronically overweight or bloated one? Which supplement is the best for the picky eater or useful to improve flexibility in the chronically stiff horse? These are all real scenarios that are encountered in daily practice. One point of view is simply to throw up your hands and say, "That's the kind of horse I have, so live with it." Another approach is to seek advice from the "convenience vendors" as I call them—those peddlers who always have the latest breakthrough product that can be fed to any type of horse and cures a long list of ailments. My complaint with these people is that they accept no responsibility whatsoever. There is no evidence to validate their claims, no attempt to ensure product purity, no warranty for effectiveness, and no interest in encouraging a diagnosis or analyzing the current diet. The Food and Drug Administration deregulated supplements in the 1980s and, since that time, they have exploded into a multi-billion-dollar industry. There are thousands of products and vendors to help you quickly part with your money.

The feeding of supplements is a function of four things. First of all we feel guilty if we think we are not doing all we can for our horse. This is a prime target of advertisers to make you feel guilty if your are not providing the best to your trusted friend. Second, it is a prevalent opinion that our present state of agriculture is inadequate at bringing to the "training table" all the nutrients that the equine athlete needs. Hay is grown on depleted soil, storage causes deterioration of the product and grain

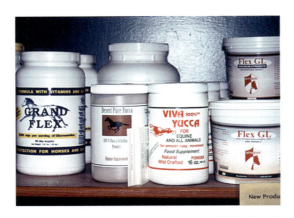

Some of the many choices of joint supplements.

nutrients are depleted through steaming, crimping or other processing. So we must supplement to make up for the deficits. Third, is the stretch of logic principle. If a scientific investigation on some metabolite turns up something positive that can be remotely applied to the horse, then it suddenly turns into the claim of scientific proof. Can we really push the metabolic machinery to produce more serotonin for our brains by providing excess thiamine? That's an unsettled question that leaves the door open for speculative commercialism. Fourth, is the competition rule; no one wants to be outsmarted by the other competitor. Because of this, anything that is promoted as giving an edge to a competitor must be purchased and added to the feed regimen. The end result of all of this is that some of the feed regimens I see are frighteningly complex. But try to eliminate something from the feed cart and an overwhelming wave of guilt and fear stops one from doing so. The opposite feelings occur when another new product is added to the feed tub. The best method of pursuing supplementation is first to get the best diagnosis possible of the condition you want to address. Then supplement for a reason.

I look at the individuality of each horse and am of the opinion that most of them have weaknesses in one or more areas of their genetic makeup. How skilled are we at filling in the gaps? There are many products available; we just have to figure out what works. Who, then, is in the best position to help you? At the risk of self-promotion, I believe your veterinarian should be the ultimate source for advice on the matter of nutritional health. Because there are so many claims regarding health benefits, he or she is the one with the greatest body of knowledge regarding physiology, pathology, and biochemistry to help you evaluate the claims and guide you in your choices. The veterinarian cannot be there on a daily basis to inspect the feed and the horse, but regular examinations and consults allow you both the ability to fine tune the nutritional and other medical requirements of the horse. If your veterinarian chooses not to become directly involved in nutritional issues he or she is still best able to guide you to a reputable nutritionist. There may well be benefits hidden in the myriad over-the-counter products, but it is a buyer-beware world with little guidance for the consumer and few regulations for the peddlers.

Let's take a brief look at some of the major categories of supplements:

Vitamins: They are essential for health and, as previously stated, the methods employed to grow and process our agricultural products definitely leads to a loss of vitamin content. But horses are able to manufacture all of the necessary B vitamins in their large intestines. There are times, however, in my judgment, where demand exceeds production. Therefore, I recommend feeding vitamins. Also, injectable vitamins have a transient, but uplifting mental effect on many horses. Which one is the best? There are several good brands. Unfortunately, you will have to do some math to determine the cost per dose. Some vitamin products list many ingredients, but the amounts are so small on a per feeding basis as to be of negligible benefit.

Fats: They are a great source of vitamin E, which acts as an antioxidant—particularly essential for newborn foals and pregnant mares. Fats also provide essential fatty acids that aid healthy cell functions; improve skin and cell membranes; increase oxygen consumption, energy and metabolism; increases kidney, nerve and immune system functions. Flaxseed is a great source of the Omega 3 fatty acids, but cooking or at least soaking the flaxseed is necessary to make it digestible. That is why it is often added to hot mashes in some parts of the country. I recommend fats for these reasons as well as the energy value for many hard working horses.

Glucosamines and Chondroitins: These are very popular, and almost everyone seems to be feeding one brand or another. I cannot comment on whether one particular brand is best, but I recommend them as adjunctive to the injectable products available. Arthritis is a major cause of disability and lost work time in the human work force. Consequently, this area of research in humans has become the focus of great attention. The jury is still out, but there are some positive results in some human studies. If we can safely extrapolate human studies to the horse, then oral supplements of these anti-arthritics may become a standard in feeds.

Electrolytes and Minerals: For most hard-working horses, one to three ounces of electrolytes per day can be added to the ration. You will need less if you use a pelleted concentrate that has salt added. Salt blocks also are acceptable, however, there are those horses that develop a craving and consume the entire block in a few days. If your horse has a tendency to "stock-up" in the legs, excess salt may be a contributory factor, however, it is commonly stiffness of the limbs or simply a lack of exercise.

Hoof Supplements: There are many reasons why horses' feet deteriorate during training, but they do. Some horses with terrible feet seem to get by just fine with no supplementation. But when horses have problems with this important part of their anatomy I think supplementation is warranted. There has been a great deal of research on the best combination and amount of biotin, methionine, sulfur, zinc and lysine. There is also significant variability in the quality of these essential nutrients as found in different commercial products. Reputable dealers with good quality control are your best bet when choosing this supplement.

Probiotics: These are friendly microorganisms that help the digestion process by breaking cellulose down into fatty acids (essential for energy). Some examples of these helpful organisms are lactobacillus acidophilus and lactobacillus bulgaricus most commonly found in yogurt. I have had horses show improvement in their look and a reduction in their gastrointestinal problems while using these. I also use them preventively after long-term antibiotic treatment or colic surgery to help rejuvenate the gastrointestinal tract. For this reason, many vitamin preparations now incorporate some lactobacillus culture into their preparations. But, remember, improper storage and handling could easily inactivate the cultures making the extra cost wasteful.

Calcium: Calcium is a mineral that makes teeth and bones hard, helps muscles and the nervous system work properly and aids in blood clotting. I recommend calcium supplementation for young, growing horses, those in rehabilitation for fractures and those with some chronic arthritic conditions.

Coat Conditioners: The argument goes that what really makes a horses coat shine is good grooming. Within a stable with the same grooming practices, there are horses with shiny hair coats and those with not-so-shiny hair coats. There is an individualization of uptake of nutrients and response to environmental factors. Consequently, there is a need to individualize the nutritional needs of the animal. A well-groomed, glossy coat has a positive psychological effect indicative of good health when the horse is being presented for show or sale. If you have ruled out all other reasons for a dull coat, try a coat conditioner for 30 days, then evaluate the results. It appears to me that rice-bran products, which are high in fat content, put a good shine on a horse.

There are literally hundreds of other additives alone or in combinations. So how do you know when you are wastefully duplicating sources of protein, vitamins or electrolytes? How do you know when you are dangerously oversupplementing or creating combinations that precipitate in the intestine and fail to be absorbed? First of all, read what you are giving and get advice when you do not understand. And second, try using complete rations so you can avoid multiple supplements. And, as stated, only use a supplement for a legitimate reason and then re-evaluate after a period of time to see if you have "fixed" the problem.

Luckily, most of the math of nutrition has been taken care of for us. Look at the ingredient list of a bag of pelleted grain ration, it is a very long list. What the manufacturer does is purchase a variety of grains depending on prevailing commodity market rates and formulates a pellet of a defined digestibility percentage, protein percentage, fiber percentage, etc. They must be depended on to use only good quality source products, not moldy, stale grains. They also must be able to provide a palatable, consistent product with each bag. This is one good reason to buy both hay and grain from reputable dealers and use complete rations rather than trying to formulate your own.

THE HERBAL CRAZE

Another facet of the FDA's deregulation of supplements is the unprecedented rage in herbal remedies and supplements. I maintain quite frankly that anyone who claims that herbs are natural is misrepresenting the truth. Any concentrated form of an herb given to effect a specific physiological condition is simply an unpurified form of medicine. Grinding up discarded shark carcasses and feeding them to a horse is not natural nor is grinding yucca into a palatable powder to consume as an immune stimulant or anti-arthritic. In addition, there is nothing inherently safer or superior about using herbal remedies. Purity is a real concern with these products. A recent California study of over 200 traditional Chinese medicines destined for over-the-counter human sales, revealed 47 percent of the products to contain active pharmaceutical ingredients or unacceptably high levels of heavy metals. The point of contention here is not one of efficacy, but one of truthfulness. Have you ever wondered why Cuban cigars are so expensive? The reason is that years and years of careful cultivation in a perfect climate coupled with proper knowledge of harvesting, curing and rolling the cigars has made them the smoothest, most consistent smoke possible. In that context, what most people get for their money when buying herbs is poor quality or completely bogus products.

❖ *THE SIX PRIMARY RESPONSIBILITIES FOR CARE OF YOUR HORSE*

1. Provide fresh water in a manner that encourages drinking. Adequate hydration is critical to performance and health. Pay careful attention to how much your horse drinks, especially when traveling, and keep the water and feed buckets clean.

2. Provide quality hay.

3. Provide enough concentrate to supply demands for energy.

4. Use limited supplements and know why you are feeding them.

5. Conduct a regular review and observation of the diet and the horse's eating habits and general health.

6. Give regular attention to proper grooming and stabling practices.

If you can accomplish this, then there is no need to fret or to feel guilty. Just enjoy your horse knowing you have done all that is necessary for a fit and healthy companion and competitor.

There are two main reasons for the surge in herbal sales. Number one, of course, is convenience. No doctor, no prescription and unfortunately, no diagnosis is needed to obtain them. The second, of course, is that even with conventional medicine, a good diagnosis is sometimes difficult to come by. And when conventional medicine has reached its limit and your problem is not solved, you have nowhere else to go except the "alternative route."

It is the challenge of medicine to improve and expand its level of diagnostics and treatment. And it is the challenge of alternative therapy to come under greater scientific scrutiny and prove the mechanism of its claims. As an example, is Arnica gel better at relieving muscle soreness than menthol and salicylic acid, the ingredients found in common liniments? Is tea tree oil better at wound healing than polysporin cream? Is Ma Juong better for respiratory problems than Tri-hist powder? Both contain ephedrine as the active ingredient.

I recommend caution when using alternative therapies in place of proven and acceptable forms of therapy. I have no problem using the aroma of elm for a horse that is "overwhelmed by the rigors of travel" as long as it gets 10 liters of intravenous fluids first. I trust the fluid therapy in guarding against the real dangers of colic and shipping fever that accompany travel.

Because, as a vet, I am used to seeing the profound effects of refined pharmaceuticals, there is a different set of rules, often intuitive rather than deductive, that guide my perceptions about these herbal additives. But, it is easy to be misled by intuitive thinking, extrapolation and faulty science. You have to adopt the rule of watchful skepticism. In other words, for each individual I try to prove to myself that the same supplement is doing its job just as it did for the previous patient.

Horses are hard to experiment with. They are as difficult as working with babies or with bizarre neurological cases. That is why the rule of the individual must be invoked. That rule states that a great deal can be learned from careful observation of one individual and then extrapolated and tested on the next individual. In this field we will never have all of the scientific studies and proof that we would like, and even those kinds of studies do not guarantee 100 percent efficacy in 100 percent of the patients. Therefore, the method of study is one of valid observation being retested time and again in other individuals. Sort of like the test of time, faulty methods generally do not hold up to this test while those that have some validity tend to persist over time. ▮

Conditioning the Dressage Horse

Dr. Hilary Clayton
BVMS, PhD, MRCVS

ROBERTA WELLAS

Dr. Hilary Clayton is a professor at the College of Veterinary Medicine at Michigan State University. She is the first incumbent of the McPhail Dressage Chair in Equine Sports Medicine. A native of England, Dr. Clayton received her veterinary degree from Glasgow University in 1973. For the past 15 years she has been a teacher and researcher at veterinary colleges in Great Britain, Canada and the United States. Dr. Hilary Clayton is one of the top researchers in the field of sporthorses. Formerly an active competitor, Dr. Clayton still rides daily using her own horses to work on innovative methods of conditioning that will improve performance and enhance soundness in equine athletes. She is the author of the book **Conditioning Sport Horses**.

Most injuries occur because of fatigued muscles. Studies have shown that in human athletes, strength training can prevent 50 percent of all sporting injuries. When muscles and tendons are strengthened, they will protect the joints against injury by stabilizing the weight-bearing column. And that goes for equines as well: if your horse is in good shape, injuries are less likely.

Also, since collection is the key for the dressage horse, fit muscles will be stronger, and holding the intensity of collected work won't be as difficult. If you haven't taken the time to get your horse properly fit, by the end of a long dressage test your horse will have trouble maintaining collection. Add to that mixture the vagaries of weather (hot and humid) and less-than-ideal footing, and you have a recipe for disaster. You need to have your horse as strong as possible so he can rise above some of these difficulties inherent at competitions. Without strength in collection, your horse will fatigue easier, the brilliance of the movement will be lost and your dressage scores will suffer.

WHY ISN'T REGULAR DRESSAGE TRAINING ENOUGH?

Normal dressage riding does improve strength, for sure. But if you can find ways to augment strength, then it's going to benefit both performance and soundness. Strength training isolates the muscles that are specifically important in the sport and then works on those targeted muscle groups. And what would those muscle groups be for a dressage horse? Who knows? We really don't know enough at this point, but as time goes by, I hope we'll get into tests that will let us better identify the target muscles. Given that we don't know exactly which muscles are used specifically in dressage, what we try to do is analyze the movements of the sport and use other exercises that mimic that movement. In other words, you use the same movements of the sport (such as piaffe or half steps) but you use them differently in a manner that applies progressive loading—increasing the amount of that type of exercise—beyond what you'd do in your normal training program. (For example: a few steps of piaffe followed by a rest. We'll get back to that in a moment.)

WHAT IS INTERVAL TRAINING?

Interval training is a training method in which high intensity activity is followed by a rest interval. Let's use the piaffe example above as the strength training exercise. Say your target was to do 50 steps of piaffe total. Rather than do the steps in one fell swoop, treat them like sets or repetitions: 10 steps in five sets—much like you'd do at the gym. By having the rest

Right: The type of strength needed at the lower and medium levels is very different than at the upper levels. The legendary Gifted and Carol Lavell.

CLIX PHOTOGRAPHY

interval between sets, you avoid getting the muscles fatigued and thus risking injuries. Keep in mind that the rest period is not just walking on the buckle, but it should a less strenuous form of exercise with some relaxation and suppling.

U.S dressage team coach and German Olympic medalist Klaus Balkenhol does this with his training, as do many people, but he does it very obviously, and he talks about allowing the muscles to recover. He works the horse strenuously for awhile and then just walks on a long rein to allow recovery, repeating the pattern of work and recovery. That's the essence of interval training.

WHAT IS A TYPICAL PROGRAM FOR A HORSE ON AN UPPER LEVEL CAREER PATH?

Collection is the single most important aspect in upper level dressage that leads us to develop the horse's strength. Collection is really our goal, and that involves strengthening certain muscles in the hind legs that are involved in the carrying and propulsion, muscles in the front legs that are involved in raising the forehand, and the muscles through the back and abdomen that are involved in maintaining self-carriage. For upper level horses, target the strength training exercises that develop those muscles. Transitions between and within the gaits are great for strength training. As an example, you can use transitions between collected canter and the more intense collection of the school canter. The school canter is the working/strengthening part, and the collected canter is the rest period.

The important thing to keep in mind with this training program is that when you use the exercises of the sport, the horse has to do them well before they are incorporated into a strength-training exercise. For instance, if the horse is doing the exercise with a hollow back you are training the wrong muscles. Also, be careful when using extensions as strength training. Use extensions in a transition type of format: do a few steps of extension or medium trot, then come back to collection. Even though the horse is extended, he has to maintain the self-carriage to stay up in front. It's a different kind of movement, particularly in the front legs, than a racing trotter where they just keep rolling over the legs. You don't want your dressage horse to roll over his legs, you want him to use his front legs to push the shoulders and withers upward. This puts a lot of stress on the ligaments and tendons in the lower leg.

HOW DOES INTERVAL TRAINING GET A HORSE IN TOP FORM?

Interval strength training is something to think of as an ongoing, integrated part of your whole training program, not just a technique for peaking your horse for a competition. Strength training is something you build, just as you build the levels of training. The type of strength that's needed at the lower and medium levels is very different than at the upper levels. The difference is collection. At lower levels you can use exercises like cantering up hills and jumping to develop the overall strength. But at the upper levels you need to focus on developing the muscles for collection and self-carriage.

WHICH TYPES OF HORSES CAN BENEFIT?

Because they are bred for it, warmblood breeds are best suited for the kind of competitive dressage we do today, and even though they benefit from strength training, some breeds that have not been selectively bred for dressage show even better results.

Walking on a long rein allows recovery. Robert Dover and Rainier at the 2000 Olympics in Sydney.

But you have to look at each horse individually and especially look at where the holes in his training or performances are. If there is a movement that a horse finds difficult, analyze why it is difficult. Rather than drilling the movement, see if you can find a way to make the horse stronger so that it's easier for him to do it. It's easy to blame things like this on laziness, but it very well may be a strength issue.

SPECIFIC STRENGTHENING EXERCISES

All of the transitions between gaits and within gaits are strengthening exercises. In a way, the lateral work is as well because it strengthens the leg that is carrying weight —the inside hind leg. You don't have to do strength training every day. If you're doing it two or three times a week, often that is enough to keep getting improvements in strength. You also don't want to do the same exercise every day because it stresses a certain part of the body. The way the body gets stronger is that the exercise causes a little bit of damage, and as the tissues rebuild themselves, they become stronger. You've got to allow time for that regeneration. What's important here is the balance between the amount of work and the time that you allow for the regeneration. If you do too much strength training or don't allow the recovery between strength training workouts then you're going to get signs of overuse such as injuries to tendons and suspensories, and

strained muscles. The moral of the story is to do different kinds of exercises on successive days. One day your strength training might focus on piaffe and the trotting gaits. The next day you might do piaffe and the other day you might do collected canter to school canter. Or you may choose to do collected work three to four days each week and then do something different that stretches the muscles, rather than contracting them, on the other days.

An appropriate way to use strength training is to integrate it into your normal daily training sessions. I suggest starting your strength training gradually. Start with very little and build up gradually by increasing the length of each repetition or by increasing the number of repetitions or sets. For instance, if you choose half steps, start off asking for six steps, trot a circle, then repeat. You may do that for three days in one week with a day in between. The next week do eight steps each time. What you're doing is getting the muscles to adapt to the work before you increase the workload. This is what really differentiates strength training from regular technique training. You do it in an organized systematic manner.

WHEN DO YOU KNOW WHEN YOU'VE PUSHED TOO HARD?

Make sure you examine your horse's legs at length each day. If you're suddenly seeing wind puffs or noticing any signs of tendon injury or muscle soreness, back off. Also be aware of any subtle signs of discomfort. For example, you may see a change in your horse's attitude—perhaps he's a little bit sour. If you suspect any signs of serious injury, you need to consult your veterinarian, but if your horse is a bit body sore or mentally tired, then consider giving him a few days off. After the rest period is over, start with what I call "active rest" such as hacking out or riding in a more relaxed frame for a week or two.

One of the things to be aware of in strength training is that your horse is not getting fatigued—fatigue is your enemy. When your horse is tired, he'll compensate by using different muscles, and he won't do the exercise properly. But, also, fatigued muscles won't protect the joints properly, so the risk of injury is increased. Fatigue shows in decreased performance. If you notice this sign, stop your work by trotting on a relaxed rein, cool your horse down, and put him away.

When properly used, interval training is a very useful tool. The benefits aren't just in a stronger happier horse, but in increased dressage scores as well. ▮

PART 2

The Rider

What You're Getting Into

LESLIE WEBB

JANE GRAY IMPRESSIONS

Leslie Webb has the unique achievement of breeding and starting her Trakehner gelding, Hannabal, and training him to FEI level almost exclusively on her own. The pair have won United States Dressage Federation Horse of the Year awards at most levels. In 1995, she competed in the US Pan American dressage team winning both the team and individual silver medals. She gives clinics throughout the United States and produced a three-part training video of gymnastic exercises. Leslie lives in Bakersfield, California, with her husband Tom and son Tyler.

So You Want to be an FEI Level Rider

Before you think warmblood, shadbelly or canter pirouette, think dedication. Whether your ultimate goal is getting to Grand Prix, pursuing an Intermediaire I Championship or training overseas, commitment is what upper-level dressage is all about. The training, the show season, the competitions, the championships . . . they really do become your way of life. That's why being a top rider can be so tough and can mean such tough choices. For example, I'm very competitive, but my son and husband come first. This often means passing up competitions and training opportunities, and it occasionally has meant putting family life on hold. When I went to the Pan American Games, for example, I was away from home for 10 weeks! Was it worth it? You bet. But that didn't make it any less difficult.

There are setbacks along the way. Financial fallout is one. Competitive disappointment is another. It is a cold, hard fact that someone out there is always going to better than you in the show ring. You won't always be a champion. And then there's your horse. If you set your goals too high and cut training corners, he can burn out. He may not have the right stuff after all to fulfill your dreams, or he may go lame. It can be devastating to train for years only to have him pull a suspensory ligament on the eve of a really big competition. You're not only looking at months of down time while he heals, but many more months of rehabilitation and schooling. There's also the chance he may never be sound enough to show again.

So look deep inside yourself. If you're up to the challenges of international-level training and competition, then go for it. But if, in your heart of hearts, you just want to be an amateur rider and have fun, then fun is what it should be. You may realize, like many people, that it's really the training process you love—taking a young horse and bringing him along to be the best that he can be—and you want to ride dressage without ever entering a show ring. I have several very talented students on very nice horses who have no desire to show—that's just not what they want, and I admire them for knowing that.

General Advice

Let's say you buy a Second Level horse with unlimited potential. Believe it or not, he's almost the smallest part of the equation. Here are other things to consider: It's almost impossible to teach a young horse new movements when you don't know what they're supposed to feel like. If you've never done the upper levels, find a trainer with FEI experience. If you don't, you'll go at your young horse's training blindly, and make mistakes you may or may not be able to fix. You can't believe the subtleties of timing the upper-level half halt or getting a horse to come through and sit down with power and impulsion all the while staying light in your hands, let alone teaching him to do flying changes. Any one element can go wrong and create a time bomb that's going to blow up in your face years later.

A good trainer will not only know the movements, she'll know how they fit into the progression of training from year to year. In the end, she'll save you time, money and frustration. Before you commit to her, however, make sure you trust her judgment, the two of you can communication openly and that her lessons are within reach of your pocketbook.

If your trainer has a schoolmaster so much the better. You can experience first-hand the movements and what they feel like, and you can practice doing them. In fact, the more horses you ride at any level, the better. Every minute you spend on top of a horse makes you that much better a rider.

The next most important individual in your support system is a good groundperson. Your trainer can't always be there, and you'd be surprised how long it will be before you can tell if your horse is absolutely straight or your position is correct. Look at the top European riders. They never get on their international horses without dressage masters watching them. We don't have a lot of dressage masters in this country, but a groom or a knowledgeable friend (I depend on my most experienced student) can stand by and tell you that your shoulder-in isn't quite on three tracks or that you're tipping your upper body in your half pass, and in the end, keep you from making a lot of training mistakes.

Find a system and stick with it. There are many different paths or languages to training a dressage horse. I don't think any one way is right or wrong as long as you choose it and commit to it because it's very hard for a horse to jump from one system to another. For example, I have my system down to a science. I know all the building blocks and steps I need to bring a young horse along. More often than not, when I take a Third or Fourth Level horse in training, I have to go back and start at the beginning and work through each step so he knows my basics and understands how to communicate in my language.

Sticking with a system also applies to you. I find it very frustrating to teach a student who's gone off and learned contradictory techniques or philosophies from someone else, then come back and had them not really fit in with my program. It's just very counterproductive for everybody.

Fact: This sport is very expensive. If you truly want to make it to Grand Prix and beyond—to international competition—you will need sponsorship (that is, unless you've already won the lottery). To travel from California to the USET headquarters in Gladstone, New Jersey for the Intermediaire I Championships, for example, you have to fly yourself, your horse and your groom. Add in the hotel, rental car, entry fees and meals, and you're looking at $12,000, easy. To add insult to injury, all the while you're off competing or training, you're producing no income. In effect, these jaunts are costing you double! So here's a tip: Start building a sponsorship portfolio now. Keep show records, articles about you, notes on big-name trainers you take clinics with and especially all your year-end standings and championships. When it's time to start looking for sponsors, you'll have something to show them.

Get into the system. Familiarize yourself with the USA Equestrian, FEI and USET rules. Know the USDF rider awards that are available. Go for your bronze, silver and gold medals. Acquaint yourself with officials at the top like show managers, judges, technical delegates,and directors of USET, USA Equestrian and USDF. And talk to Grand Prix riders. Some of them will become your competition, but they'll still be your best allies and a terrific source of information.

Listen to your horse. Train on his schedule, not by the calendar of championships and selection trials. I've found that most horses are comfortable progressing at about a level per year. If you push faster than that, and if you're lucky, you miss steps or mess up training basics (ones you'll have to spend twice as much time filling in or fixing). At worst, you'll risk your horse's mental or physical breakdown.

Here's what I do to keep my horses sound and happy. Depending on the weather and the show season, I work my young Training through Second Level horses five days a week. All my other horses I ride six days a week because the older the horse, the more he needs to keep moving, and the less time he stands in his stall, the better. I usually give my horses Sunday off. Monday I devote to long-and-low or putting them on the longe line. Tuesday I work in the dres-

If your goal is to have fun, than that's what dressage should mean to you.

CLIX PHOTOGRAPHY

sage arena on basics. Wednesday, Thursday and Friday, I school. Why three days in a row? I learned the hard way that working them hard one day and light another made them shut down on the second day at multiple day competitions. They were looking for their light day! Saturday is another long-and-low day, this time out of the dressage arena in a big field near my house or on the trail.

After a show, my horses get at least two days off, and every Thanksgiving we have the "Webb Olympics" when we play games on our horses. Keeping fun in the picture makes the whole thing worthwhile for all of us.

❖ A WORD ABOUT FITNESS

As a rider, you're going to need more and more muscular and aerobic fitness as the levels get more difficult. Consider adding gym workouts to your riding sessions, especially if you only ride one horse a day, and absolutely if you hold a desk job. I ride at least four horses a day, but I still work out in the morning. Here's how I look at it: Every trot stride equals a sit-up. If you can't do 200 sit-ups with ease, how are you going get through a dressage test without falling apart?

Monitor your horse's soundness. Remember, he needs to last for years. He doesn't need to show in five classes a day. He doesn't need 90-minute hard schooling sessions. He does need the best footing you can possibly school and ride on. He does need proper hoof trimming and correct shoes. And he does need regular veterinary care. Have your vet check his soundness, tendons and flexibility every month or six weeks—or as often as your pocketbook will allow—with a physical exam. An ultrasound at the same time may seem like a luxury, but it will confirm that there's nothing developing on the inside that will turn into an injury weeks or months later.

Be a smart competitor. Show at least a level below the level you're schooling. Don't show any level until every test of that level is 100 percent at home (If you don't have the flying change called for in Third Level Tests 2 and 3, for example, you have no business riding Third Level Test One). Read your tests and keep track of your scores. Judges don't all agree, and some judges are tougher than others, but test scores are the best gauge of when you're ready to move up (usually when you're consistently achieving mid-60s) or when something's very wrong (usually when you're scoring consistently in the 50's). While judges can't instruct you in their test comments, anytime a judge points out a problem, try to talk to her (check first with the show management!); she may be willing to share some helpful hints about fixing it.

Always look your best. Good turnout reflects good training and seriousness of purpose at any level. Remember, first impressions do count. Even at the lower levels, a clean coat, clean breeches and neat braids are the first thing a judge sees. Just because you're riding Second Level and not Prix St. Georges doesn't mean your braids can be three days old and sticking out in all different directions, and your boots can be dusty and your saddle pad stained. You may not be able to control the shy in the corner, but you can always control your boot polish!

Finally, make sure your neat turnout is also appropriate. If you ride in a snaffle at Fourth Level, wear a hunt cap or a bowler. You haven't earned the right to wear a top hat until you put the double bridle on. And once you do start using the double bridle, wear spurs—that way you'll be better prepared for FEI classes that require them.

What to Expect at Each Level

Second Level: At this level, concentrate on straightness, balance and impulsion. When you ride a straight line, are your horse's haunches following his shoulders? Is he honestly on your inside leg and outside rein? Will he show you that he's through the back and not behind your leg by readily moving forward when you put your leg on? Will he come back when you half halt? And will he do it in all the movements? If he doesn't jump forward in the shoulder-in when you put your leg on, he's not ready to do shoulder-in in the show ring. Forward and back are basic responses that must be 100 percent confirmed at home before you even think about going to a show, because they're what create that very bold test you want to ride when you're in front of a judge.

Midway through your Second Level year, start your Third level movements such as your half pass work. Start making your counter-canter circles smaller. Be sure you can move your horse laterally in both half pass and shoulder-in position and that he can responsively go from lateral movements to being absolutely straight. Introduce what I call baby or half steps during your upward and downward transitions between walk and collected trot. These steps—only ask for one or two—should feel very powerful as your horse sits down more and lifts his shoulders higher, because they'll eventually turn into piaffe.

Start single flying changes too. Remember, though, that flying changes (along with piaffe and passage) are movements where you must never punish your horse no matter how badly he executes the movement. If you punish him, he'll just become afraid and will never try again. It took me an entire year to teach Hannabal how to do a correct flying change. I would get so upset when he couldn't figure it out, but he was really trying hard. Punishing him wasn't the answer because it would have said stop trying. I just quietly kept going and one day, all of a sudden, it happened—a clean, forward, very expressive change exactly where I wanted it. From that day on, Hannabal has always had changes that are 100 percent and very expressive.

Third Level: Once again, be 100 percent confirmed at all the movements of this level, particularly in the flying changes, before you start showing. However, the only fudge factor I allow: as long as the changes are 100 at home, it's okay if they lack a little polish in the show ring. Your horse's straight line may be a little wobbly, he may swing his haunches a bit or he may lose impulsion—that's okay as long as he's confident.

The increased demands of Third Level make it a good time to remind your horse about a fundamental element in my training program—response time. Whether you put your leg on him, give a half halt or push with your seat, his response should be almost instantaneous. In fact, at this level, it should be approaching 100 percent. If it's like a distant echo, that's not good enough.

After all, if he can feel a fly and wiggle a muscle to get rid of it, he can feel your aids and respond just as quickly. Anytime you allow him to ignore your leg or respond slowly to a half halt, you're allowing his basics to slip away.

Make time to watch the "big guys" ride. I never miss an opportunity at a show to sit at the competition arena or the warmup area. At home, since I don't have a regular coach and do most of my schooling on my own, I watch videotapes of the World Cup, the World Championships and the Olympics. Then I compare them with tapes of me schooling or riding a test to see first-hand whether or not I have enough collection or a big enough trot or enough bend. It's one of the best ways I've found to sharpen my eye and to fix problems.

Fourth Level: This is the time to think about musical freestyles (once you get to FEI levels you can't do without one) and your double bridle (optional, but preferred by 99 percent of riders at this level). Start getting the feel of riding with four reins the way I did—by adding an extra set of reins to your snaffle for several months. When you do begin using the double bridle, make sure your trainer or a knowledgeable friend helps you pick the right size curb bit and bridoon and is there to help fit them. You can really confuse or frighten your horse if they're incorrectly adjusted. I remember the first time I used the double, I thought the curb was hanging too low in my horse's mouth, but it was absolutely correct.

For your first ride in the double, go out on the trail or pick one of your long-and-low days, not a schooling day, and let your horse get completely comfortable. Drop the curb rein completely and don't even touch it. When you do pick it up, you'll be astonished at how your horse reacts. It's like putting power steering and power brakes on a car that's never had them.

What should you be schooling? Tempi changes with 8 to 4 and 3 strides between. Cantering down the centerline (now that your horse has to enter the arena at the canter instead of the trot), canter/halt transitions and cantering nearly on the spot for four or five strides to start preparing for your canter pirouettes. Once he can do that, all you have to do is add a little turn and there's your quarter pirouette, soon to become your half pirouette then your full pirouette.

There's not that much difference between Fourth Level and Prix St. Georges —just more tempi changes, more collection and a longer test. So if you're really comfortable and successful at Fourth Level, it's perfectly acceptable midway through the year to add some Prix St. Georges and get a bit of FEI competition under your belt. In fact, study all the FEI tests up to Grand Prix so you start to know your final destination.

Prix St. Georges

Again, start the year at Prix St. Georges, make sure it's respectable, and toward the end, try some Intermediaire I.

When your horse feels ready, start schooling two-tempis, full canter pirouettes, and the zigzag at the trot. Remember though, this is no time to lose sight of the purity of your basics. Make sure your horse stays soft in the mouth and balanced, with an impeccable response time.

Your baby or half steps should be getting shorter and shorter, with more cadence, loft and suspension. Start schooling and preparing for passage and piaffe, which require at least a year-and-a-half of schooling before you think about showing them. If possible, have your trainer get on and teach them to your horse. Believe me, he'll be much more confident learning these movements under a knowledgeable rider.

INTERMEDIAIRE II AND GRAND PRIX

Your big goal in the first year of each of these levels is to keep your horse fresh, happy and fit, and to not worry when you don't even come close to the 65 percent you're hoping for. Your horse has to want to go into the arena because the work is fun and he enjoys it, and if you start getting extremely demanding and overschool the movements, he'll shut down or quit during competition. Just try to make the first year a pleasant and happy experience for your horse and be happy when you get a 60 percent. He'll start getting really comfortable with his job and knowing exactly what he needs to do, and that's when you can start asking for boldness.

❖ THE STEPPING-STONE HORSE

In the hunter/jumper world, people think nothing of learning what they can from a horse, selling him and stepping up to a more advanced horse. In the dressage world, people either want to have their Grand Prix horses now or they want to advance their lower level horses well beyond those horses' capabilities. The result? Timid or over-horsed riders struggling to sit on big, extravagant movers, or talented FEI-caliber riders plugging away on hopelessly limited horses.

TIPS FOR SUCCESS

1. Get a trainer.

2. Become familiar with the tests.

3. Watch and listen at shows.

4. Develop a good eye, and you'll become a better rider.

5. Stay in shape—both of you!

6. Keep a sense of humor.

7. Enjoy what you're doing, if you're not happy, your horse isn't happy.

I truly believe that the world of dressage needs stepping-stone horses—lower level schoolmasters. There is no shame in learning all we can from a horse and then selling him. Indeed, you should be happy to see someone else learning from him. That may, in the end, be his higher purpose—to teach. I, for one, am looking forward to the day when my FEI horses are ready to be sold to Young Rider candidates so I can watch those riders have their turn at learning and succeeding! ▌

The Psychology of Climbing the Levels

DR. TIMMIE POLLOCK, PH.D

A licensed clinical and sport psychologist in private practice in La Jolla, California, Dr. Timmie Pollock specializes in working with riders to help them identify and remove blocks to success, improve performance and to increase their enjoyment of competitions. She is a member of the American Psychological Association's Division of Sport Psychology and the Association for the Advancement of Applied Sport Psychology. An active dressage rider and competitor herself, Dr. Pollock joined the California Dressage Society in 1968 and has served as chair of California Dressage Society's San Diego chapter.

I've been fortunate to have worked with several U.S. Equestrian Team long-listed riders in dressage as well as a few international-level jumper riders. What I have found is that advanced riders seem to intuitively know about and use "mental skills" such as goal-setting, visualization, positive self-talk, how to concentrate, etc. They are already pretty good at controlling show nerves. In contrast, the lower level rider often does not know what the skills are, let alone how to use them. And as most of us are aware, the more average rider frequently struggles with performance anxiety with varying degrees of success.

I worked with some of the long-listed riders before the 1996 Olympics. Next to coping with the high level of stress, one of the biggest challenges for these riders seemed to be dealing with the politics of making the team. Reactions to the realities varied from experiencing personal conflict to feeling fear of becoming a target for criticism and negativity of others. It takes a really tough competitor to make it at these levels and that includes finding the strength and resilience to regroup whenever faced with new, unexpected challenges. The work with some of the riders included values clarification. A few made the decision that the price was too high personally for the potential benefit. They discovered that making the team wasn't worth it to them, and it wasn't why they rode. They were okay with redefining their goals. You may reach the same crossroads in your career and decide to pull back and be satisfied with where you are and how you fit in to the whole scheme of competition.

Another problem often encountered by serious riders is "the slumps." These riders will go through periods where they're not performing at a level they know they are capable of. Sometimes, but not always, this may be accompanied by a lack of motivation or boredom. It can be a tricky thing to sort it all out and to come up with a solution. A sport psychologist with "clinical" skills can help a rider sort out possible causes. For instance, the slump could be related to life-stage changes where the rider is reassessing life goals: Where are they going and why? For instance, what if the rider has fallen in love and decided marriage and family are now important? How do they fit that in with competing?

A slump also can be the result of training too hard for too long with not enough reward. This is classic burnout and happens when what you put into something is less than what you are getting out of it for too long of a period of time. Depression can even be a result of burnout and will affect both confidence and motivation. In addition, a normal drop in performance happens temporarily any time you change something significant about how you do what you do. This is part of the normal learning process.

Something that you need to consider as you move through your riding career is what kind of price you are willing to pay for success. What can you do to keep your sanity as you're moving through the levels? Are you willing to have the mindset that lets you go after this sport and get it any way you

Our relationship with horses sets our sport apart from any other. A jubilant Klaus Balkenhol with the legendary Goldstern at the 1996 Olympics.

CHARLES MANN

can? That may or may not be okay as far as being consistent with your belief system.

Success can only be defined by the individual. What is success to you? Does it mean making the Olympic team? Does it mean that you know how to ride and train lots of different horses? Or is it knowing you know how to ride and train one horse to Grand Prix? Or is it knowing you know how to train any horse to Second Level? The inability to succeed comes when you're not clear about your goals. Let's face it, most people aren't going to make the Olympic team—-there are only four spots every four years, usually filled by the same people, so that really moves your chances down. Get really clear with yourself about what is a realistic version of success for you and find out what would make sense to you as a worthwhile goal.

The confidence level of a person is really important when it comes to success. Confidence only can come when you're clear about your goals, your values and the knowledge that you're making progress in some way, and that you like who you are and you like what you are doing.

Get clear about your goals by sitting down and thinking things through. Think about what goals are possible. Look at each goal to see what it would take to reach it. From there, ask yourself if you're willing to put in the time and effort to reach this goal: Are you willing to pay that price? If the answer is no, then choose another goal and then look back again. Keep looking and find out what really would make you happy and feel fulfilled. I've noticed with some elite athletes, not just riders, many of them aren't doing their sport just for fulfillment or happiness. They do it as some sort of challenge or to prove something. This seems to work for them. Let's face it, it's not just perfectly happy, healthy people who achieve a high degree of success such as making the Olympic team. There are a lot of people who are on a mission. They may say, "Damn those people who were always criticizing me.

I'll show them." A good friend of mine says, "If we all had a perfect childhood, none of us would do anything extraordinary. We'd have nothing to prove! We'd probably just be ordinary, average people living ordinary, average lives and be happy with that." Sometimes these other "agendas" work better in motivating some people to great success. But it's a narrowly focused drive—like a dog snapping at your heels: "I'm not going to have relationships. I'm not going to have fun. I'm not going to take vacations. I'm only going to focus on my goal." They have a willingness to sacrifice everything to an extreme. Now, having said that, while the focused drive and willingness to sacrifice is necessary for success, I don't think this almost masochistic attitude is necessary. And what I see more often in those who are truly successful is a more balanced personality with the ability to sustain a focused drive for long periods of time. It is very possible and desirable to achieve goals while deriving joy as well as a sense of accomplishment from the process.

As a psychologist, I also come at the angle of mental health when setting goals. You don't want to have your life totally out of balance. Very often, when a rider reaches her goals, she gets a feeling of what now? What's next? A lot of Olympic athletes talk about the horrible anticlimax that happens once they've reached their goals. There is even a support group for ex-Olympians because they often go into such a crash afterward. Athletes now try to find some purpose in life after the Olympics. Their

Top riders are willing to make sacrifices to attain their goals. Ask yourself what you are willing to give up to reach your own. Isabell Werth and Gigolo at the '96 Olympics.

CLIX PHOTOGRAPHY

entire lives had been filled with their sport, and now what? So many Olympic athletes are so young and they have their whole lives ahead of them and they don't know how to refocus and move forward.

The sport of riding differs from other sports in a couple of ways: It's the only one where men and women can compete against each other on equal terms. It's also one of the few sports where you can compete at any age—you're not washed up at age 25. You can ride dressage for a lifetime, and that can take a bit of the pressure off, but it can also lock you into a life pattern, continuing to let you live your life off balance. If you're 25 and in another sport where age matters, you know you're done: You can go ahead and get married, have kids etc. If you're 30, and you think you can still go for it, but only if you give up everything else, you're more likely to do so.

One difference in our sport is the relationship with the horse. How many people have a love for their tennis racquet? Not many compete to show the world what an incredible golf club they have! Think about how much motivation comes from the love of your horse. Many riders I talk to feel that it's almost a duty to a particular horse to let that horse shine. They feel an obligation to ride the horse to the best of their ability for the horse.

One of the great things about riding and competing in any sport, and that includes dressage riding, is that in order to be at all successful, people invariably must come up against themselves. It's a perfect opportunity to learn plenty about who you are. You'll notice the same patterns in your riding as in your life. For example, if you have problems with a short temper, or if you get easily discouraged, or if you look to others to provide motivation, these will be apparent in your riding as well. In order to be successful in your sport, you will need to address and overcome these traits. Many riders will have the motivation to keep taking that challenge and confronting parts of themselves. The results of this personal work will then generalize to the rest of life and things will go better there as well. To me this is such a positive way of looking at the process of achieving mastery in any area of your life. ▐

Advice for the Dressage Rider

KLAUS BALKENHOL

STACEY SHAFFER

German policeman, Klaus Balkenhol, first appeared on the international dressage scene with his police horse, Rabauke. However, Klaus is best known for riding another police horse, Goldstern, with whom he won two Olympic team gold medals and one individual bronze medal. He also won the team gold medal and individual silver at the World Equestrian Games in 1994. Together with Goldstern, Klaus has retired from the police force, but it does not mean that retirement means rest. Now he has a chance to train and work with his horses full-time. Klaus is now the coach for the U.S. Dressage Team.

A horse is always a horse, and a rider is always a rider. What I mean is that a horse is himself, first and foremost, and that a rider must always consider him and make the horse a priority above his training. His well-being must always be in the foreground of everything the rider does. Above all, a rider should be a horseman first.

A rider always needs help from the ground; it's never perfect. My most important priority is to hone the understanding between horse and rider. A good trainer must feel the horse and always be a good rider. ❚

Rider Opportunities

Sharon Biggs

Learning Opportunities Abroad

It's easy to envy professional riders; they ride as if they are part of the horse. They do make it look easy, but so would you if you could ride all day, every day and on different horses offering different challenges each time you rode. But like most riders, you've most likely got a full-time job and full-time responsibilities.

Wouldn't you like to have a chance to really hone your skills, to give yourself a chance to ride different horses or even advanced horses? Wouldn't it be great to feel what it's like to do a flying change or a canter pirouette? Or maybe even spend a week with your own horse with nothing on your mind but learning new skills?

Places like this really exist for riders of every level and discipline—amateurs and professionals alike.

Karen Lancaster started Cross Country International (CCI) 10 years ago because she was looking for someplace to go to progress her riding. "I went to jumper rider Tony Hill in England, and I rode four hours a day every day. It was like an intensive language course. My riding progressed in leaps and bounds. I started CCI soon after to offer similar opportunities for other people. There is a lack of standardization of riding instructors in the United States. It's not to say that there aren't good instructors. I think there are some great instructors here in the US, but there is just no common standard." Top-level instructors rarely have time to take on a novice pupil. In Europe, riding stables are extremely competitive, so top instructors such as brother and sister Christopher and Jane Bartle of Yorkshire Riding Centre, both national dressage champions, will happily take on novice students.

All of the courses offered at Cross Country International are taught by British Horse Society (BHS) certified instructors. The BHS is the national governing body in the United Kingdom for recreational riding, riding schools, teaching qualifications and dressage. It is respected throughout the world. In fact, CCI offers a credentialing program for those who are interested in obtaining this teaching certificate.

"We guarantee that everyone has a great instructor. Our instructors take everyone on a case-by-case basis. When we book the person, we take down the rider's age, weight, riding history and goals. The instructor is prepared for the rider's situation. Generally speaking, 90 percent of our clients improve greatly after one week at a training program. Our clients are training with someone who is top in their field and who understands that he or she is working with an amateur rider. The trainers are not going to be frustrated that this person is never going to the Olympics. In fact, many of our instructors say the more novice the better because you can get so much out of a novice rider in a week. Most intensive-training-program riders are professional people—amateur riders who ride on the weekends and after work."

Can you bring your horse? "It's difficult to bring a horse with you overseas, however you can bring your horse to our New York facility. But the point is that you are there to learn from an educated horse and to get a feel from a horse that has the skill. Most facilities have numerous school horses to choose from." CCI's academies have more than 30 horses of every level in each facility and are all well-mannered. But don't assume they are the slow, pluggy variety of school horses that you learned to post the trot on in your early days. These are well-trained schoolmasters used to help lower-level dressage riders improve. Advanced riders shouldn't feel left out either; there are plenty of facilities with horses for them. "I've sent several Grand Prix dressage riders to Christopher Bartle because he has wonderful advanced horses and, of course, excellent ability to teach the riders." ∎

One Rider's Experience in Europe

KASS LOCKHART

Kathleen Lockhart currently teaches classical dressage riding to professional instructors, adult amateurs, and children from beginner through Intermediaire I, and trains horses through these same levels. She has trained with several nationally and internationally known dressage in-structors, most recently Melissa Simms, Head Trainer at the Reitinstitut von Neindorff in Germany (1991–present). She holds a USDF Silver Medal and in 1995 was Reserve Champion at Prix St. Georges at the Southwest Dressage Championships.She has written many articles on training methodologies for popular riding magazines, including a series, "The Psychology of Training," for **Dressage and CT** *magazine. She is a graduate of the USDF "L" training program for judges.*

REITINSTITUT VON NEINDORFF

I wanted to go to Europe to study because I had been riding for a number of years in clinics. I had a talented horse, but I couldn't seem to press beyond Second Level. I tried to address that issue in every way with every clinician I rode with. They were vague in their answers, but they did say it would be best if I received intensive instruction. I decided that the only place I could get that was in Europe.

I had heard about Egon von Neindorff through an acquaintance who had lived in Germany. She went to a performance at the Reitinstitut von Neindorff, and she spoke very highly of the school. I had ridden in a few clinics with Erik Herbermann (a former student of von Neindorff's) and he spoke well of the school. He told me that there was an American woman there with whom I could possibly ride. He later asked that instructor, Melissa Simms, if it would be possible for me to contact her regarding riding at the school, and she said "yes."

I made my first trip to Germany in 1991. I've either returned to the Reitinstitut or worked with Melissa in California for a month every year since then. Melissa also comes to conduct clinics at my barn in Texas two or three times a year.

I wanted to learn how to become an upper-level rider, but I discovered I was very naïve about that. I wanted to show at the FEI levels, and I hoped that by going to Europe, I would begin to get an idea of what I was missing and how to go farther in my riding. I could, before I left for Germany, ride all the upper-level movements, however I didn't have access to trained horses, and I hoped to be able to ride some there.

Well, I got to ride advanced horses all right, but I couldn't ride any of them! I assumed I would be able to ride the horses but thought perhaps I might be unable to ride a canter pirouette. As it turned out, I couldn't put a single horse on the bit. At first, I thought that they were giving me these awful horses that nobody could ride. Then I saw other people ride those same horses and they looked beautiful. I saw Melissa herself riding them, and they looked elegant, relaxed and supple. Then I thought, well it's just these horses that act this way, but I can ride my own horses. I realized after a couple of trips, that the problem lay in my own riding. As I learned to ride the horses at the riding school better, my own horses at home began going better as well. I came to understand that horses will get used to anything you do, but that doesn't mean it is correct or that they will be optimal performers because of it.

LESSONS LEARNED

I was introduced to a proper system of riding. Only by getting out of the clinic format, getting intensive instruction and being able to ride properly trained horses could I do that. In Germany, training style varies by the school and the instructor. Most riding instruction there takes place in group lessons. You're expected to just ride the horses and to not require intensive one-on-one instruction, though, the first year, I had a lot of private instruction. I also rode in quadrille quite a lot. That was helpful and interesting to me because I could concentrate. The horses at the riding school are so experienced that they will do all the movements, especially in quadrille, while they might not be so willing if you are in an arena by yourself. In quadrille, they know what they are doing, and they just do it. This was a blessing for me because I got a feel for the movements, and I didn't have to be exactly right.

The eye-opener for me was this: All the riding techniques that I had been taught in the past weren't working with the school horses. The teacher/student relationship wasn't so personal that I could ask any willy-nilly question I felt like. What I did was sit and watch Melissa and her students ride, watched her teach lessons all day long and I took notes. Then I took my lessons: I got lunged, I rode in private lessons and I rode in quadrille. I was forced to make changes because I couldn't get the horses to go forward and I couldn't get them to come on the bit. The first week I was there was a total disaster. Melissa worked with me on the lunge a lot since the key to all my trouble was position. When my position improved, things started to work.

I went back to the school the following year because I felt I had been exposed to something special. I felt that I had a glimmer of something that I had known was

Kass Lockhart riding the Andalusian stallion Alamarante at the Reitinstut Von Neindorff.

COURTESY OF CASS LOCKHART

there because I had read about in books. I could see it at the riding school, and I wanted it. The issue of becoming an upper-level rider is not the issue for me anymore. I've done that. I was Region 9 Reserve Champion at Prix St.Georges in 1996. That year I was able to take a horse that was a successful upper-level horse not performing at his potential and make him better.

My goal now is just to become the best rider that I can be. There is just so much to learn. A whole lifetime is really not long enough. In a sense, I gave up what seems now a rather narrow goal (riding and showing at a certain level) and adopted a much larger one—one not limited by the constraints of the show ring.

There is a myth that every German rider rides wonderfully. In reality, the average German rider looks pretty much like the average American rider. There are really good German riders and really awful German riders, just as there are both good and bad riders here in America. People have expectations about what the German training is like, but that varies by school. At von Neindorff's the trainers are never rough with the horses. I never saw them use the whip in any way other than as an aid—including in the airs-above-the-ground movement. The whip was most often used to tap or stroke. The horses there were expressive, lively, and full of animation and their own personalities—-not in any way cowed or overly submissive. The riding was never "strong" riding.

Research any potential riding school carefully and with whom you are going to ride. Don't go over to ride with *Bereiter* "So and So" and find out you're riding with his working student. That happens to a lot of people. It helps if you have a recommendation from someone so you can get hooked up directly. You also have to make sure that the school has horses for you. Many private trainers don't have school horses and so you'd have to bring your own horse. Von Neindorff's is a riding school and not a show barn. He has around 70 horses, with at least 50 of them working at Fourth Level standards, and many of them working at FEI standards. I think it's an optimal situation to be in because you can have a wide variety of horses to ride—different conformations, different breeds, etc., to experience what sorts of problems present themselves to you. You'll also have the opportunity to see many horses being schooled daily in piaffe, passage and airs-above-the-ground, and the quality of the collection is extremely high.

The problem in America is that there are very few places where you are going to find 50 horses that are all trained to Fourth level and above. Von Neindorff's also has horses that were brought along to Fourth Level standards and then allowed to specialize in what they are good at. If the horse is good at flying changes (maybe he can't piaffe but he can do one-tempis), then that horse would be a master at one-tempis. When you started one-tempis, that was the horse that you learned on. The teacher could pick a horse that could help you. The horse I learned flying changes on was an old Lipizzaner gelding that had been used in the quadrille performances for years. That horse did flying changes when I came to the right place in the arena. Even if I didn't give him the correct aids, he still did the change. Then I graduated to other horses that I had to be a little bit better rider, and then a whole lot better rider to get the change, or to do it correctly and not have the horse run away with me on the other side of the arena! There is such an opportunity to learn so much about riding. Also, it helps to go away from your own home turf and your own horses, because, almost always, you and your horse have an agreement as to what is acceptable, but that may not necessarily be correct. ∎

Becoming a Professional Rider

SHARON BIGGS

CREDENTIALING

In some countries, such as the United States, anyone who knows how to saddle a horse and put their heels down can print up some business cards and go into the horse business. Of course this can be a good thing for someone who has been around horses all her life, or maybe spent several years as an apprentice at a famous trainer's barn. It begs the question: What would a credential add to her life? Olympic dressage rider Steffen Peters is one such rider who does not have credentials. And that's no mean feat when you consider that Steffen comes from Germany, land of the very old and esteemed *Bereiter* system. This certification system requires the candidate to apprentice at a riding academy for three years, earning a small stipend of around $300 per month. Steffen chose a different route: "I worked for Jo Hinneman for six years and I went to an academic college. I think the proper education is very important regardless of whether it's theoretical or practical education. However, I don't believe in proving that knowledge by doing a cer-

tain test. If you can bring riders and horses to the upper levels and you yourself are competitive, I think those are the credentials that are important." British expatriate, Anna Burtell, now based in Magnolia, Texas comments, "Unfortunately, for us lesser mortals, we don't ride as well as say someone like Steffen Peters. There are few really good riders and even fewer really splendid riders. If you can have some sort of credential to back you, you'll have something to fall back on; something to give the public a way to find you. Credential programs also help you understand safety and give you building blocks to create a system of teaching."

Anna holds the highest accolade awarded in the very prestigious credentialing system of the British Horse Society called the Fellowship of the BHS. There are only 55 members worldwide holding this credential. This particular license helped her get jobs in Singapore and Dubai, but when she moved to the United States, she says that the credential really didn't help her get her current job because as no one in the United States knew what it was.

California dressage instructor Holly Shane is currently working toward her

A student takes a moment at a competition to help out.

CLIX PHOTOGRAPHY

United States Dressage Federation (USDF) instructor certification—a fledging program designed to test trainers on their training and instructing skills. Her goal is simply to learn a better way of teaching and training and not to use the certificate to obtain more students. "I've found that getting students is really a matter of luck and networking," she explains. "I go to every single USDF seminar for my own education rather than for the business the credential may or may not bring."

Trainer Vicky Baker from Virginia sees things a different way. Initially she chose to go after her certification through the American Riding Instructors Certification Program (ARICP) mainly for the insurance discount, but she soon found out that there was much more to the program. "I found that parents of my students were respecting me more after they found out that I had a credential. If they had problems with a lesson or with some safety issue, I could tell them that this was the approved way of doing things." Through ARICP, Vicky learned a better philosophy of business planning and safety, but most of all her own teaching style jelled for her. She was able to organize her thoughts and teaching plan to better assist her students.

To credential or not to credential? That is the question. It is an interesting topic and one that has spurred several heated debates between many a trainer. Consider the options and find out if credentialing is the right thing for your own business.

PROS

• Insurance can be up to 15 percent cheaper, according to Equisure Insurance Company, for those instructors holding BHS or ARICP credentials.

• You will learn a system of teaching or find a systematic way of organizing your own teaching style.

• Your name will be registered at the association, and anyone who researches will be able to find you. The American Riding Instructors Association has a Web site with instructors' contact information.

- You will learn safety management.
- It shows your customers that you are proven against a standard.

CONS

- Insurance may not be a factor for you if you live in a zero-liability state such as Virginia.
- You've worked for years learning a style of teaching, and you're not interested in learning another.
- You and your students are doing well and have won awards in your specific discipline.
- You're well known in your city, and your client list is full.
- The monetary investment needed for the credential is not worth it for your own business.

THE WORKING STUDENT EXPERIENCE

Dressage riders are all hungry for knowledge. Some of us have gone so far as to volunteer for less-than-glamorous duties just to be able to soak up knowledge from top trainers or breeders. If you cannot imagine spending any time shut inside away from horses and are dying to find out if you've got what it takes to become an equine profession-al, consider becoming a working student. You can apprentice overseas or as close to home as swapping a few hours of work for a lesson from your local instructor. Whichever option you choose, becoming a working student is an incredible way to start your journey down the path to becoming a professional or toward simply becoming a better rider.

Laura Forrester, a 23-year-old architecture student at California Polytechnic University, spends her summers and vacations exchanging work for lessons. Being a cash-poor student she found that a working student position was the only viable way to continue her equine education during her college years. "My responsibilities can be summed up as a sort of "right hand man." Basically, I pick up the loose ends. I tack up horses, lunge them, put them away, groom at shows and offer moral support whenever needed. I also help my trainer on the ground while she's riding. An extra pair of trained eyes is really important in dressage." In exchange for Laura's work, she gets several lessons per week and the opportunity to ride well-trained horses.

Barbara Werbach, a former small-animal veterinary technician was on burn-out when she decided to give up regular employment and go to work, full time, for her dressage trainer Kass Lockhart of Dallas, Texas. "My main responsibilities are to have the horses ready when Kass is ready to ride and then cool them out and bathe them. I receive a lesson each day."

WHAT'S IN IT FOR ME?

Hands-on experience is irreplaceable. Some things just aren't taught in school or in a one hour weekly lesson. Consider the fact

❖ FERRETING OUT OPPORTUNITIES

1. Find equine professionals by looking in your local feed and tack stores and yellow pages for addresses of stables and local equine organizations. Ask your current professional if he or she would be interested in swapping a bit of work in exchange for lessons and information. Ask to help in any way: pulling manes, lunge-ing, help on your instructor's days off, etc.

2. For more formal programs, check in national magazines or trade journals. Organizations or individuals usually advertise in the classified section. Also, national organizations, such as USDF and the USA Equestrian, are gold mines of opportunities for such programs. Here you can get names of breed establishments and trainers to contact.

3. A bit of self-promotion can go a long way. Consider placing an ad in a trade journal or magazine requesting a working student position. This way you will have interested parties contacting you.

4. Approach trainers at horse shows.

5. Offer to volunteer at shows. It's a great way to make contacts.

6. Scribe at dressage shows. This is another great way to make contacts and get an educational experience as a bonus.

that you'll have a mentor—someone to go to for advice. You'll also get to ask loads of questions, learn professionalism and find out how a successful business is run.

Barb Werbach found that "the most valuable experience is being able to work with and ride a lot of different horses. Each horse can teach you something different." Laura Forrester agrees, "To become a confident, responsible rider, you must be able to ride experienced horses. It's difficult and nearly impossible as a recreational rider to be able to have horses like that at their disposal. You'll find a lot of well-trained horses at a professional's stables."

Being an working student will help give you a foot in the door of the industry. When you emerge as a hopeful professional, you will have your boss's name attached to your resume. You'll also have made valuable contacts in the horse world.

SURVIVAL TIPS

"Keep the lines of communication open with your trainer. Listen and observe as much as possible while others are taking lessons and the trainer is working different horses. Ask questions and have things clarified if you do not understand. Be flexible. Expect to be an improved rider with a better understanding of horses. Sometimes the hours are long and the weather isn't the best, but think of your long-term goals."

– *Barbara Werbach*

"Make the long hours and lack of salary bearable by focusing on being able to ride experienced and upper-level horses. Also, be totally willing to do anything. Be honest, reliable and responsible. Once you've earned the professional's trust you'll get to do more."

— Laura Forrester

WORKING STUDENTS IN EXCHANGE

If you long for the down-under pastures of Australia or perhaps like to ride across the heath in England, then the Communicating for Agriculture Exchange Program may be for you. CA has a successful 12-year-old equine exchange-program for those wishing to work overseas. Barbara Nelson of CA explains, "The equine program is limited to 100 apprentices per year. We match young Americans, 18 to 28 years old, with host families from other countries. England and Australia are our main countries, but we also place in Denmark, Germany and other European countries." The responsibilities are varied depending on what type of training you are interested in. You will receive room and board with your host family plus a monthly stipend of $300 to $500. Participants pay a program cost that includes air transportation, administration fees, health insurance and a one-year CA membership (Costs range from $1,800 to $4,200 depending on the country. Some grants are available.) To qualify for the program you must be single with no children, have a valid driver's license and have the abil-ity to cope with the difficulties that arise when working in another country. You also must have at least one year of practical experience in your chosen field.

Apply for the program by phoning for an application (800) 432-3276. Send a video of yourself grooming a horse and riding. The director of the program will assess the video and send it to the appropriate country for approval.

FINDING TIME TO RIDE

Horses and jobs don't really go together. A strange statement you might think, but let's consider it: You have to work in order to pay your horse's way, and you have to have time to ride the horse, but your time is eaten up by your work. And what about finding time to show? And for that matter, what about finding time to practice for said show? How about taking off work to show? See what I mean? Even if you don't have the "traditional" nine-to-five job—say you're the one responsible for taking care of the house and family—you've got spouse and family making demands on your time.

Most people don't often choose a career with horses. There are loads of dressage riders out there with training and showing ambitions, but where do they find the time to fit it all in? This rider has down the art of marrying work with horses.

Crystal Choate of San Diego, California is a seventh-grade English teacher working from 7am to around 4pm Monday through Friday. She worked full-time as a teacher's assistant to put herself through school and as a school janitor during the summer. Crystal works one hour from her home, but she lives only minutes from the stable.

Crystal started taking lessons in junior high school (her mom gave up bowling to be able to afford lessons for her daughter) but started paying for her own lessons at the same time she was putting herself through school. A die-hard horse nut, she yearned for a horse all her life but was only able to swing it through a fluke. A girl at the barn had lost interest in her horse and was looking to place him. This horse turned out to be the very horse Crystal had yearned after for years. Payments were arranged for the cash-strapped ex-student, and soon Crystal was holding onto the lead rope of her very own horse. Her mother, recognizing the fact that Third Level dressage horse Kasanova would probably be her only grandson, arranged a "baby" shower for her daughter. The gifts from this party filled Crystal's tack box.

"I leave at 7am and work my eight hours-plus, fight traffic to the stable, and change into my riding clothes in the outhouse. It's dark and full of spiders! I can't tell you how many socks have gone down the outhouse. Then I ride and get home at 8, I fix dinner, eat and go to bed. The next day I do it all over again. Saturday, however, is riding day. My family and friends understand that all plans must be scheduled around my riding. They understand that this is my lifelong dream.

"I've certainly had to make sacrifices. First of all there is my truck—an '89 Chevy S-10 pickup with a recalled paint job! I don't know how many times it's broken down on me. I'm on intimate terms with Triple-A. I have to live with roommates—I can't afford a house of my own—so I have to live with Dungeons and Dragons gaming geeks and cats that I'm allergic to. The way I look at it is that no matter how expensive the horse is (payments, plus board, plus expenses equals $750 per month) it's a whole lot less expensive than therapy. This is seventh grade that we are talking about here, and although I love them to death, they are a handful. My goal isn't showing, but to become the best rider I can be."

TIPS

1. Always have a pair of socks at the barn in case you wore stockings to work that day.

2. Have a coin jar handy on your dresser to collect money for extra supplies.

3. Let it be known to your family members that there are certain times for your horse. Set a time!

4. Have playtime with your horse —don't make it all work.

THE ADVANCED YOUNG RIDERS PROGRAM

It is said that our future lies with the young. Although that quote was probably

The top four young riders from the nine USDF regions are selected to compete at NAYRC. Scores are based on a horse-and-rider average score at Young Rider qualifying competitions. Each horse-and-rider combination must compete in the FEI Young Rider Test (counts for 60 percent) and the FEI Young Rider Individual Test (counts for 40 percent) at three qualifying competitions (Two AHSA "S" or FEI judges must preside). They may compete in four competitions and drop their lowest score (minimum scores of 55 percent are required). At the championship, two members from each team ride the team test on Thursday. Friday, the next two ride. The top three scores from each team are averaged and gold, silver, and bronze medals are awarded. Scores are ranked and the top-12 riders ride the FEI YR Individual test. Riders who don't place in the top twelve compete in the Consolation Class and ride the FEI Young Rider Preliminary Test.

Each team usually has fund-raisers to help defray the cost of showing at NAYRC. There is a $400 entry fee as well as the added costs of housing, transportation, uniforms, etc. In addition, each horse is required to have a passport, and riders are required to jog their horses before the FEI vet—just like their adult counterparts. The Young Rider program is governed by the USDF, USA Equestrian and observed by the USET. Thanks to Howard Simpson, coordinator of the Young Rider program at Tempel Farms, and to the USDF for the preceding information.

meant for society at large, it is also an apt expression for the future of dressage in the United States. The Advanced Young Rider Program helps prepare young (ages 16-21) dressage riders for the North American Young Rider's Championships (NAYRC). Each championship includes teams of the finest riders from United States, Canada and Mexico (Eventing and show jumping are held at the same time.) This program is duplicated all over the world on every continent. However, the main goal of this program is to nurture the tender talent of this country's best riders in hopes that they will continue on to represent the country in bigger international competitions as well as to carry on the sport of dressage.

Nicole Perry tried out for Young Rider Region 7 team in 1995 and 1996, and made the team in 1996 (tenth individually and team gold), 1997 (sixth individually and team gold), 1998 (silver individual and team gold), and in 1999 (individual bronze and team bronze). Today she trains out of her home stable Patchwork Farms in El Cajon, California, and competes with her

Young Rider mount, Masterpiece, in Grand Prix. She competed on Guenter Seidel's former Pan American Games horse Batido at the 1999 NARYC. Her goal is to help other Young Riders who are dreaming of landing a spot on an NAYRC team.

"I grew up watching the Young Rider program, and I always wanted to be part of it. Competing in open FEI classes is a difficult thing at age 16 [due to their experience.] You want to be competitive but showing against the open riders is pretty much impossible. The Young Rider program gives riders a chance to jump into the FEI levels without being over-faced and overwhelmed.

"The first year we won the gold medal was the most special for me. We had a few problems in the team test, but even though we had our problems, the team came through to win. It's an incredible thing when you all work together for each other. All year we are competing for ourselves, but when we get to the championship, we work for and with each other.

"When I first started, I was competing with other riders and trying to be as tough as they were, always comparing myself to the quality of the best. I learned a lot because I had someone to compare myself with. The Young Rider tests [the team test is a tougher version of Fourth Level] are diffi-cult enough so it really makes you learn how to ride and get through them. At the Championships I learned that there are a lot of good riders from all over and that I shouldn't get so self-involved.

"It was just like a mini Olympics. Once you finish the vet jog, the U.S. Equestrian Team gives you the Young Rider badge to wear, which is a version of the regular badge. We get to wear the badge until we get our regular team badges. It was exciting when I got the USET badge. In fact, it was the only thing I wanted!

"When you ride, you go through phases. Young Riders got me through one phase and now I'm trying to go out into the open classes. Young Riders got my name out there nationally. USET let me go out into the Developing Riders Program—for open USET riders. It's usually for people who've done Miller's qualifying classes. Usually Young Riders are not invited to go, but USET thought my talent and Louise [Labrucherie's] were good, so they let us go.

"Through one year's championship, I got some scholarships from people who donated money and would like to see me go on. If it weren't for Young Riders I wouldn't have been able to get those kinds of opportunities." ∎

Avoiding the Frustration Trap

DR. TIMMIE POLLOCK, PH.D

The one common thing that every dressage rider has, no matter what level, is experiencing feelings of frustration—that horrible emotion that robs us of our peace of mind, sends us heading to the couch with a jumbo size bag of M&Ms and sometimes, causes us to dabble with the idea of nailing our spurs to the wall—forever. That's it, cancel the lessons and the tailcoat fitting, and that bank account marked "horse" can now be spent on a vacation to Tahiti. Frustration can creep up out of nowhere and when you least expect it; perhaps in the middle of a warm-up ring when your horse shies at a piece of paper blowing by. Suddenly you hear these words from inside your head, "He's going to do that in your class, and you're going to look stupid, Stupid. Why do you even bother? Obviously, you can't control him." Suddenly, a simple harmless shy turns into a major turning point in your riding career. It's an insidious emotion and has, does and will continue to affect every dressage rider on his climb to reach his summit of goals. No doubt about it, frustration can derail the hopes, dreams, and aspirations of many talented riders. And the unfortunate truth is that it probably has claimed many already. If this sounds familiar to you, you may be heartened to know that this emotion need not rule your life. You can learn how to avoid the trap of frustration, and in turn, set yourself up for success instead of failure.

I'll help you learn how to recognize what kind of thinker you are, how to monitor your thoughts and how to set realistic goals for yourself. Success is an attitude—a good one in which there is no room for negative self-deprecating thoughts.

A VERY SPECIAL SPORT HAS VERY SPECIAL FRUSTRATIONS

Imagine you're a tennis player getting ready for the big game. You pull your trusty racquet (the one you've spent years saving up money to buy and even made a special trip to Europe to purchase) out of its bag and begin to warm up. Much to your dismay, the racquet decides it doesn't like the color of the line judge's shirt and decides it will jump out of your hand each time that judge walks by. It's all you can do to hang on to the thing. Also, since you're nervous, your

1. List three negative self-statements you might make about yourself.

2. List three negatives you might say about your riding.

3. Identify three negative self-statements you find yourself making.

4. How can you challenge these? Identify the "untruth" and replace it with a truth.

5. What thoughts do you have before competition?

When entering a show:

On the way to a show:

At the show:

After your class:

After the show:

6. What are some of the ways you could improve your confidence through self-talk?

7. Devise a plan for the next month or time period before your next show for you to improve your self-talk.

Example: In the next month I will do the following to improve self-talk:

tennis racquet picks up on your feelings and goes all saggy and soft as you begin your game. It's impossible to make it through one round. Sounds a bit farfetched to the tennis player that this scenario will ever happen, but if you substitute "horse" for "racquet" you can get a pretty clear picture of the special circumstances the sport of dressage throws our way. The bottom line to this story is to realize that this is a difficult sport you've chosen—one in which you have little control. The answer is to find a way to deal with the frustrations that go with having little control over something like a shy. And a shy is one thing, but what about other problems that riders encounter?

Many professional riders live in fear that the promising horse they are riding, the one they've poured so much time and training, and don't forget emotion, into will be pulled out from under them by the owner, die of colic or fall victim to an injury. How many times have you heard at shows, whispered around the grounds, something like: "Her horse developed navicular." All eyes look down at the ground as the unlucky rider approaches. It's a horrible frustrating thing that can happen to a rider, and everyone prays that it doesn't happen to them.

Amateur riders have their own kettle of fish. They are spending money on their training, possibly family money and, in some cases, obtaining home-equity lines of credit in order to be able to finance a horse that they can learn on. Many amateurs have trouble finding the time. They have kids, husbands, full-time jobs and other demands of their time. Frustration rears its ugly head when something goes wrong during their rationed hour of riding. They want their session to be perfect: after all, they have little time and what they have has to be spent in quality time. The flip side is that some find that they haven't the time and so, why should they bother? They sell themselves short and

don't push themselves to achieve any goals.

We could go on and on with the frustrations that plague us; it could be something as simple as learning to make a good 20-meter circle, learning to sit the trot or perfecting a canter depart. Whatever it is, I'm sure you've identified your own personal snafu and are ready to learn how to turn the frustration around.

WHAT TYPE OF THINKER ARE YOU?

The way you think has a strong influence when dealing with frustration. Negative thoughts actually affect your health making you feel weak and unable to tackle the task at hand. On the other hand, changing your negative thoughts to positive can give you peace of mind and freedom from self put-down.

The first thing you must do is to identify what type of thinker you are. This will have bearing on how you'll change

Success is an attitude. Leave no room for negative thoughts. Individual medal winners at the Sydney Olympics. Anky Van Grunsven, Isabell Werth, and Ulla Salzgeber.

CLIX PHOTOGRAPHY

Take a moment before you ride to focus on positive thoughts. A helper gives you extra breathing room.

CLIX PHOTOGRAPHY

thinker has a good handle on controlling frustration. Studies have shown that the difference between top athletes and average ones is that the top athletes never recognized "failures" as failures but rather as learning opportunities. These are the aspects of the optimistic thinker.

Negative thinkers tend to think an incident is permanent. One mishap can change the future of their riding career forever. The explanatory style of the negative thinker is a downward spiraling one—one in which one bad thought leads to the next until he is convinced that the incident is his fault and he can't do anything to change it.

You can also be a mixture of both types of thinkers, which is where most people fit in.

DEFINING SELF-TALK

Those words you hear in your head each time you ride or embark on any endeavor is self-talk. For instance, if you are feeling a bit stiff one day and are having trouble sitting the trot, you might say to yourself, "Well, I'm stiff today, but I'm not always. I'll loosen up in a minute. If I don't, tomorrow is another day." The negative thinker would say, "I'm so stiff, I'm bouncing all over the joint. Listen to my saddle squeak. My poor horse. Why do I insist on torturing him? He should have another owner." Basically, self-talk is the difference between being nice to yourself and being really mean to yourself. Consider it this way: How

your thought patterns. There are basically two types of thinkers: optimists and pessimists. Optimists have a different "explanatory style" than a pessimist. (An explanatory style is a way of explaining what happened.) Optimists will realize that the incident was just that—an incident. It's temporary and out of their control. "These things happen," is their motto. They also tend to be more humorous about the mishap than a pessimist. This type of would you want your best friend to talk to you? Would you want her to put you down and yell at you, or would you rather she support you and help you?

The one thing you have absolute control over is your thoughts. In this respect you have the power to control your own future. Start becoming aware of what you say to yourself as you ride. Jot down these statements later and consider them. Are they real or are they blown out of proportion during the heat of the moment? One way to get a handle on negative self-talk is to challenge it—replace erroneous thinking with realistic truthful thoughts.

The next thing you need to do is to learn to reframe your self-talk. This is much like challenging, but instead of writing down the statements and coming up with new ones, you will be reframing thoughts as they occur. Let's take the example of the horse shying that we used in the beginning of this chapter. Instead of saying to yourself, "I can't

Use your trainer as a sounding board for whether your goal and the time you've set for yourself are realistic.

CLIX PHOTOGRAPHY

Set attainable goals. Not everyone will reach the giddy heights of an Olympic Championship. Isabell Werth and Gigolo at the '96 Olympics in Atlanta.

CHARLES MANN

control him, he's going to do that in a show." replace it with "Horses shy. That's part of their nature. Everyone understands that. The judge understands that. It doesn't mean a thing." You can even find a compliment in it: "I'm sure glad I spent lots of time on the lunge line. I could have fallen off if I didn't have such a solid position." You get the idea? You simply turn a negative thought around and put a positive spin on it.

If you don't think that negative self-talk has any control over you, consider this: Your subconscious mind wants to work for you, and in fact, picks up on statements you make in your conscious mind. If you think, "I always ride badly when it rains," then guess what? Your subconscious minds says, "OK, she wants to ride badly. Let's help her." Your negative thoughts soon become reality.

GOAL SETTING PUTS FRUSTRATION IN ITS PLACE

If you use goal setting as one of your tools to success, you will find that you won't get sidelined by frustration as easily. With goal setting, you have a light leading you from one step to the next, helping you understand where you are going.

Sit down and identify your goals. Maybe it's that you want to be able to ride Third Level by the end of the show season, or perhaps you set your sights on entering a certain show. Write them down on paper. Next, identify the stumbling blocks you foresee that will keep you from reaching your goal. There are two kinds of stumbling blocks: Physical and psychological. Physical blocks are those things that are real or that you think are real. Examples include a lack of time, strength, money and a good-enough horse. The second kind is psychological. These blocks are the impediments that exist only in your mind. They can be lack of self-confidence, lack of belief in success, anxiety or fears. These obstacles are no less intimidating than physical obstacles. Write down these as well. Next, identify possible solutions to your obstacles. For physical obstacles get creative. Turn to your instructor for ideas, consider finding a sponsor if money is your issue or perhaps you may need to tighten your budget to allow more money for lessons. Come up with an escape plan in case something goes awry. If your horse has to rest an injury for three months, you will enlist plan B or plan C. It's also important for riders to have goals that are separate from the ones they have for their horses. You need to know where you are going in your own career separate from your horse. To identify psychological barriers, do some reality checking with your friends and family. Talk it out with a therapist or a sport psychologist.

Your plan of action is to get honest with yourself. Are your goals realistic? Are they really worth the time, effort and money? Would you be happier finding a more middle road to travel? This is the time to get brutally honest with yourself. Of course, jot this down in your notebook too.

Finally, formulate a plan of attack. Set time parameters. Break down your goal into simple steps that make your assent easier. The great mosaic artists of Italy use many tiny pieces of material to create their huge murals. It seems a daunting task to try to make something so large out of something so small, but the artists allay their frustration by tying a string around the area they are to work on that day. They only work within that string. They know that tomorrow they will be tackling another section and, soon, the big picture will begin to appear. Think about approaching your goals the same way. Tie a string around your work and only tackle what you can tackle that day.

Learn to be happy and comfortable in your current level. By this, I don't mean rest on your laurels. What I mean is to not discount what you have achieved. In fact, as you record your goals, you will see progress written down. Take inventory of these accomplishments, past and present. Also, find out what your assets are. What is your best feature as a rider? Maybe it's that you have quiet hands or have an elegant position. Learn to appreciate yourself for these things, and try not to blame yourself for more than what's due. Avoid your frustration trap by monitoring self-talk, by challenging and reframing negative thoughts, and setting realistic goals for yourself. ∎

How to Gain Sponsorship

SUZANNE FRASER

FLYING SQUIRREL GRAPHICS

*Suzanne Fraser is the writer and publisher of **Financing Your Equestrian Activities** and **The Dressage Competitor's Handbook.** When not riding, teaching or writing, she works for an Internet company. She is sponsored by several of her riding students, family members, friends and State Line Tack. She holds a USDF bronze medal. She lives in New Hampshire with her husband Douglas and her Danish Warmblood gelding Helenikos.*

Dressage rider and trainer Suzanne Fraser found that her funds were running out long before her goals were attained. The answer? Search for a sponsor. Vermont neighbor Jane Savoie suggested ways to help her locate riders to interview who had found sponsors. Suzy learned so much during her search that her husband suggested she write a book on the subject of sponsorship.

The very thought of a sponsor conjures up the image of a benevolent benefactor handing you, a cash-poor rider, the key to your future on a silver platter. And, of course, this fictional patron wants nothing in return from you but the promise that you will always do your best. Such luck.

Sounds great but does this really happen? Not often. It is very rare that a rider can obtain one sponsor who will foot the entire bill for his climb to success. Most sponsored riders have several who help. And most sponsors do expect something back.

It is a myth that only famous professional riders can gain sponsors while obscure, talented amateurs flounder in the background. The truth is that any talented rider can secure a sponsor to help him reach his competition goals. But it also takes much more than luck. What a talented rider needs to secure a sponsor is not simple chance but what I call the five Ps: positioning (getting your name out in the community), participation (participating in equine activities), presentation (make an impressive impression on people, i.e. good manners, dress, horse's grooming, etc.),

❖ *PUTTING TOGETHER A PROPOSAL*

1. Write a cover letter. Introduce yourself and briefly tell what you've done (there will be more room to expand later on in your proposal) and what you are looking for. Make your first and last paragraphs the most important. Keep in mind that these are busy people, so make your cover letter scannable and your proposal attractive.

2. Include photos and/or a video. Make your proposal visually appealing.

3. Include separate documents on awards, certifications and competitions. Arrange these chronologically with your most recent achievements appearing first.

4. If it's money you're after, include the all-important budget proposal. Write down how much money you need and why. Be honest and realistic.

5. Include a separate sheet expanding on what you will give back in return for sponsorship.

positive attitude (no poor sports, please) and perseverance (sticking it out through the no's and rejections).

WHO CAN CONSIDER THEMSELVES SPONSORSHIP MATERIAL?

Anyone who needs money can ask, but realistically speaking, the beginner or intermediate rider is better off soliciting help

❖ FIVE PITCH IDEAS

What are your talents? What can you offer someone? Consider these options but get creative in your own pitch.

1. Find products you real like and use every day such as grooming supplies, bridles, feed and supplements. Contact the companies by sending your proposal, and tell them in your cover letter that you love their product and would like to represent them as a sponsoree. If you are not a well-known rider, settle for products instead of money. Show them that you are serious about promoting their product, wear the logo on your saddle pad, hand out pamphlets and samples, etc. They may give you money after a time. Tip: Pick an up-and-coming company that just released a new product. Chances are they will be looking for someone to promote that product or that no one has yet approached them for sponsorship.

2. Pick professionals that you use (farrier, vet, feed store, tack store) and tell them that you will refer people to their services in exchange for sponsorship. You may get money or maybe free services or feed.

3. Offer to host question and answer sessions at conventions, clinics and shows.

4. Offer your testimony for an advertisement.

5. For individual sponsors, suggest that they come and watch you ride. Play up the social angle.

from friends or family. A sponsoree ripe for the picking is someone who is skilled and outgoing, and of course, a pretty competent horseperson. Ready yourself for sponsorship by doing the five Ps we discussed before. Also, get yourself out in the community—volunteer, work at shows, run for the board at your USDF Group Member Organization. Participate in as many activities as you can and be professional. Upbeat, outgoing individuals make good representatives. Take the no's on the chin and stick to your goals. Expect more no's than yes's in your sponsor search, but don't take them personally.

WHAT CONSTITUTES A SPONSORSHIP?

Sponsorships vary a lot. Some people give money for a horse purchase. Tack stores or catalogs might provide free equipment or clothing, or perhaps a feed store will provide feed for the horse or farm. And, yes, there are rules regarding sponsorship. To find out what the current rules and regs are, contact the USA Equestrian for a pamphlet. And by the way, all sponsors and sponsorees *must* report to USA Equestrian.

HOW TO ATTRACT A SPONSOR

The most important thing to understand is that gaining a sponsor takes time, effort, patience and persistence—with persistence being the most important. Put together a proposal—a pitch that introduces yourself and outlines your intentions. In your proposal, be clear about what you're trying to accomplish. One of the benefits of a proposal is that you are less apt to leave things out, such as budget concerns, etc. You'll spell it out to yourself and to your prospective sponsor instead of blundering through an awkward phone conversation with someone you may not know.

Your next task: compile a list of people to contact. Consider individuals as well as businesses and corporations. Send out your proposal and follow up, call or arrange a face-to-face meeting. If they are not interested in a sponsoring you, ask them if they can suggest someone who might be. Remember to thank them and send a follow-up note of thanks. You never know: They may decide to sponsor in the future.

THE PITCH

In essence, ask not what your sponsor can do for you, but what you can do for your sponsor. When approaching a friend, family or riding student, their motivation in helping you comes from the goodness of their heart. Do not assume the same of strangers. They are going to want something back from you, and you must tell them what you have to offer. When promoting yourself to an individual, tell them that they will be able to bring their friends and family to see a really good horse that they own part of. Or perhaps they are horse lovers and would enjoy watch-

ing the day-to-day training, so play up that angle. Invite them to practice sessions and answer any questions they might have. For corporations or local businesses, tell them what you are going to do to promote their product, how you will improve their image and how you will be able to attract a certain type of person or customer.

Consider including non-horse companies on your list, such as food products sports beverages or energy bars. How about a health supplement or a restaurant? Horse people need to stay healthy and eat as well as everyone else.

DRAWBACKS AND PITFALLS

There are several ways that a rider can get the rug pulled out from under her. An individual sponsor might have a reversal of fortune. This is something you can't safeguard against, and it happens sometimes. Also, the rider and sponsor may have a personal falling out, which is why you must maintain a professional demeanor at all times! Sometimes riders are vague about what they need, especially where money is concerned. Many people are really uncomfortable talking about finances, but to avoid misunderstandings, both parties need to know what to expect before going into a sponsorship. Another common problem occurs when riders or sponsors aren't living up to their promises. Always get a contract. This way both your sponsor and your expectations will be spelled out. However, before

Tell your prospective sponsor about your sport and the market it produces. Facts come from the American Horse Council's 1997 comprehensive study:

1. There are 6.9 million horses in America—a rise from the two million-plus counted by a 1992 U.S. Department of Agriculture census.

2. There are 7.1 million Americans who are horse owners, equine service providers, employees, and volunteers.

3. The horse industry produces goods and services valued at $25.3 billion each year and pays about $1.9 billion in taxes to all levels of government.

4. Racing, showing and recreational riders account for more than 75 percent of the industry's total value of goods and services.

5. Horse ownership is economically broad-based with 38 percent of horse owners earning less than $50,000.

---

you sign that contract, think long and hard to decide if you can live up to your promises.

To avoid the having the rug pulled out from under you, try to have more than one sponsor. If one drops the ball, you won't be left high and dry.

One drawback many riders find is that they feel as though they are a bit "owned." Essentially they are because they are accountable to someone who is footing the bill, and one who expects results, whether small or large. However, many sponsored riders find that sponsorship is well worth the drawbacks.

MISCONCEPTIONS

Being a good rider will not bring people to your door. The majority of people need to go out and knock on doors.

When you're knocking on these doors expect many more no's than yes's and expect to work very hard at your search. It's really rare for one sponsor to pay for everything. You need to be prepared to go after a lot of different people. But you'll be surprised who'll give you money, so pitch to as many people you can.

Realize that nobody's "on" 100 percent of the time and that there will be times where you will not do as well as you would hope, so be open and honest with your sponsor. If you satisfy your sponsor and live up to his expectations and your promises, there is an excellent chance you are going to satisfy him and get continued support. I think that if more people put pressure on the television networks to broadcast equestrian events, sponsors would be more readily available for riders. ▮

PART 3

Competing

Judges' Forum

JANET BROWN

A native of Colorado Springs, Colorado, Janet graduated from the University of Colorado in Boulder. Her interest in dressage grew when she lived in England. She attended the Talland School of Equitation and took her British Horse Society Exams. She received her USA Equestrian 'r' judge's card in 1978 and was promoted to USA Equestrian 'I' in 2000. She is also a Canadian 'S' judge, an FEI 'C' judge, and an USA Equestrian Sporthorse Breeding judge. She has judged all major FEI shows in the United States, and national Championships shows around the world. As a rider, Janet earned her USDF Bronze, Silver and Gold Medals as well as many USDF and USA Equestrian Horse of the Year titles. Her students actively compete through Grand Prix, and she clinics throughout the United States. She lives in Peyton, Colorado.

PET PEEVES

I hate to see a rider lose "stupid" points by not being accurate. Sometimes a horse is being naughty or is very green and the rider cannot be accurate. But many times a rider has the possibility to ride an accurate test and she doesn't, so the rider's 8 or 9 becomes a 7.

I also think that instructors don't' teach their riders how to ride a test, how to use the corners, and how to prepare the horse for the next movement. The corners are your friends, but many riders, including FEI riders, seem to ignore them. I see horses cutting corners, haunches (and engagement) falling out, etc. Trainers need to teach their riders to ride two straight lines connected with a turning aid. If the rider never gives the horse any aids, the horse will travel the corner his own way. Then the rider tries to leg yield the horse sideways into the corner, which isn't the correct concept.

Mistakes in the half pass is another pet peeve of mine. Especially in half passes that start from the centerline, the rider often is so concerned about getting sideways that she doesn't think about the turn onto the centerline and that the haunches make the turn *after* the forehand. Riders must learn to put the haunches on the centerline, bring the shoulders in the direction of the line of travel and *then* go sideways. If not, the haunches will lead every time.

I'm also amazed how many people go off course even with a reader. Again, I don't think riders are familiar enough with the tests when they go to shows. They should know exactly where the circles and transitions are going to be made. The letters P, V, E and B sound a lot alike, and riders look at their readers like they are going to murder them. But it's not the reader's fault. I've seen several times where the wife is riding and the husband reading. She goes off course, and gives him a look that could wither a tree!

I have to blame the trainers and instructors for not preparing their students well enough. The student should be instructed as to proper dress, grooming, warm-up arena etiquette, what to do if she has an "off course" and, of course, she should have practiced the test. Why should a trainer let his student have a bad experience just because the trainer did not give her the information he needed?

Riders who come into a test with a horse that is unable to perform the test don't impress me. Everyone can have a bad day as we all know, but I'm talking about a horse, for example, in a Fourth Level test that has no bending, therefore no lateral movements, no flying changes, etc. I rode and trained several horses that could do piaffe/passage but could not do changes every stride, or could do the changes and passage but not piaffe. So I didn't show them Grand Prix because, in my mind, they weren't Grand Prix horses. However, today, it seems that some riders think it's okay to show in a level where their horses are missing a very important aspect of the test.

WHAT DO YOU EXPECT TO SEE FROM A HORSE AND RIDER?

I would like to see a horse and rider in harmony with enthusiasm from the horse. Too often I see a horse that is forced by the rider's hands or punished by the riders' legs and spurs every stride. I don't like to see large spurs on riders who have insecure seats and legs. I love to see a rider who gives the horse confidence and allows the horse to make a mistake without punishing him. The rider needs to remember that the horse will make mistakes too, and that they must go on and use it as a learning experience.

WHAT THINGS DO YOU REWARD/SCORE PARTICULARLY HIGH?

I once gave an 83 percent for a First Level ride in Washington State. The horse did not perform a flawless test, but he was a 9 mover—very elastic and expressive in all three gaits. The rider had a wonderful seat, elastic hands and a lot of tact. When the horse made a mistake, she sat quietly and let him find his balance under her seat, not pulling and using the reins.

My highest scores are for the horse and rider who are a team, moving with balance and harmony, both looking like they are having fun.

HOW CAN RIDERS IMPROVE THEIR SCORES?

First, they should know the test. They should be as accurate as possible. They should use their corners. They should make sure the horse is confident with the requirements of the test. I always tell my students if the horse can do the movement well 9 times out of 10 at home, they are then ready to show that movement. The horse and rider should have a clear concept of the training scale and have firmly established basics. The riders also should know where their horses are weak and where they are strong. Few horses can do every movement as an 8. If a rider tries to make his extended trot an 8, and the horse can't do it, he'll fail and get a 4.

IS DRESSAGE COMPETITION CHANGING?

Yes, the quality of horses has greatly improved—the horses are super. Our judges' training programs are being copied by countries around the world, and show managers are getting more sophisticated, using computers for scheduling, results, etc.

Our training is getting better, but still I think this is the United States' weakest link. We don't have enough good trainers with the correct knowledge of the basics. Riding a horse correctly from back to front over an elastic topline into a steady contact is not easy. Riders must insist that they be put on the lunge line to develop a deep and supple seat. If an instructor doesn't offer lunge lessons, a rider must find another instructor.

IS JUDGING CHANGING?

Yes! When I first started judging in 1976, it was perhaps easier. The methodology was if the horse made a mistake, the score was a 4. When Eric Lette became Chairman of the FEI Dressage Committee, he tried to put a positive outlook into the judging. He has asked us judges to be advocates of the horse and rider, and not to see ourselves as those with the power to punish. He stressed quality. We now must assess what has happened before the mistake and then give our mark; there are no more automatic 4s. This type of judging has also improved the scores around the world. The education that is available to judges now is wonderful. USDF takes judges to Europe every other year with a program organized by Marianne Ludwig. There we have the chance to watch top international horses for several days and be instructed by the best in the world. ❙

Judges' Forum

AXEL STEINER

TERRI MILLER

Axel Steiner has been involved with horses all his life as rider, competitor, teacher, breeder, and last, but not least, as a judge. As one of a handful of FEI "O" dressage judges in the world, he has judged major competitions in 25 foreign countries including sitting on the judging panel for the 2000 Olympics in Sydney, Australia. Axel is an Instructor/Examiner for all USA Equestrian judges' programs and is currently on the USA Equestrian Board of Directors and the dressage committee. He is a founding member of the USDF is a board member of The Dressage Foundation. Axel holds USA Equestrian "S" and FEI "O" judges' cards. He lives in Coronado Island outside of San Diego, California.

PET PEEVES

Many riders compete at levels that they and their horses are not prepared for. In America we have an entry system by ego and pocketbook. In other words, our riders do not have to qualify to ride at a particular level. We are one of the very few countries of the world with such a system. We, as Americans, don't like anybody to tell us what to do and, unfortunately, the losers are the horses and our sport in general. Horses often are being asked to do things that they are mentally and physically not ready to do. When potential sponsors see poor performances in the ring, such as riders bouncing or pulling frantically on the reins, we have a bad advertisement for the sport.

The root of the problem is ego, bad coaching and bad judging. The first two are obvious but the third might need some explanation. Even though our judges' education and training has become much better in the past 10 years or so, there are still some judges who either do not have a firm standard or have developed a floating standard as a situation might present itself. Often, some of us judges get to a regional championship and wonder how a particular rider has ever qualified to be there. (Unfortunately, often the riders wonder that themselves when they see the competition.) It's not fair to the riders for judges to overscore them at local competitions and then to have them be unable to match up to the competition after having spent a lot of money and time to get to a championship. The solution is more educa-

tion for riders, coaches and judges—and a removal of some judges from the system.

I don't think we should force freestyles on our riders. On the other hand, we should greatly encourage those who are ready to take the challenge. Riding a freestyle should be a privilege—it should be earned. There are several reasons for that. Freestyles are not only more difficult because riders put in combinations that are normally not found in the tests but that are still allowed, and freestyle is also the best advertising for our sport. If we want to put our sport in front of the public, we want to put our best side forward—not just somebody moving around the arena trying to do impossible things. Spectators are very good judges; they can tell if something is harmonious and pleasant to watch or if somebody is forcing something bad down their throats. You don't ever see a skating freestyle in front of spectators by ice skaters who are wobbly at the ankles. Why should we ask for freestyles by riders who are still wobbly at their levels? We should have a firmer qualifying system to make sure that only the top people get in. But, more importantly, I think we should foster the idea that freestyle is a privilege and then make a big deal about it. Then we can expect something really great. I have judged freestyles around the world, and the United States has some of the best freestyle riders in the world. Our choreography and our music are tops. The ideas and the flow are great, however, the technical part of the performances doesn't quite measure up yet, but luckily there are some wonderful exceptions.

Overschooling in warm-ups is also a pet peeve of mine. Many riders leave their best tests in the warm-up arena. Shows are not for schooling, but for showing what was schooled at home.

The quality of our horses improves constantly, but our quality of riding doesn't keep up. Riders expect the horses to perform at peak levels but they themselves can't sit the horse or often are generally out of shape. We all know that horses are athletes but few riders behave like athletes. The cure includes self-discipline, which can translate to many hours on the longe line. And even our top riders need the occasional longe line session.

WHAT DO YOU EXPECT TO SEE FROM A HORSE AND RIDER?

Riders should be prepared, mentally and physically, to do their best. They should show at a level below what is being schooled at home. Riders need to read the purpose on the top of the test sheet and understand what it means and to be able to translate that purpose into their own training. If riders can't fulfill those requirements in a satisfactory way, they shouldn't show at that level.

Know the test. Yes, it is permissible to have a reader, but a rider is ultimately responsible for his or her test. Knowing the test makes a rider much more confident. I also expect the turnout of the horse and rider to be of high standard. If nothing else, they should be clean and tidy. First impressions are important.

WHAT THINGS DO YOU REWARD/SCORE PARTICULARLY HIGH?

I reward the quality of gaits and quality of riding together with the throughness that is required for the particular level with a submissive way of going. The test should look easy and look like fun. The rider not only has a major influence on every movement, but the rider also has a major influence on the collective marks. I think that's a fairly large part of the test that's often overlooked. The rider can influence the gaits. If the horse has a good walk and it's not very active, the rider can make sure that the horse moves in a more active way, and he'll receive a higher score. Through the rider's influence, impulsion improves. Sometimes a rider can make a horse look better than he really is by giving the appearance that he does everything possible for the horse in the arena. That will certainly endear that rider to me, and I will give him the higher score. On the other hand, if I feel that the rider is impeding the horse, then the rider will get, deservedly, the lower score.

HOW CAN RIDERS IMPROVE THEIR SCORES?

Riders can improve their scores in many ways! Ride a test as written and be accurate. Pay attention to transitions. When a rider enters the arena, he should halt at X—not three feet before or three feet after. Be straight. When taking a turn at C, don't start at I, but come closer to C and make as tight a turn as required in the test. Don't avoid the corners: They are a rider's friends because they provide the opportunity to make quick corrections before going on to the next movement. Corners are "free areas." In the corners you can make corrections (within reason), and it will not influence the score. It's what a rider does as a result of the corner that will influence the score.

Be accurate. If the test reads shoulder-in from B to F, start at B and finish at F. At home a rider might ride a shoulder-in through the corner, but that's not what is asked for in a test. If there is a lengthening that is required, get moving within a reasonable distance from the letter. If medium or extension is asked for, get moving at the letter and show a clear transition at the arriving letter. Transitions are very important but still largely ignored by most riders. Also, never make a judge guess. We usually guess low.

IS DRESSAGE COMPETITION CHANGING?

Yes. Horses are better and are much more bred for the sport and the task at hand.

They are bred smaller and are therefore better suited for women riders. The sport has been changing from a male dominated sport to a female dominated sport in a very short time period. Even though we have a way to go, riding has improved from what it was 20 or 30 years ago.

IS JUDGING CHANGING?

Yes. There is more and more education. We are constantly learning and understanding biomechanics. Because of that, sometimes we have to reassess our previous learning. We now have nearly worldwide standards. Obvious nationalistic judging—judges who support their own countries—is fast becoming extinct. Judging is much more out in the open. At some championships, every score given for each movement for every rider is made public. The press gets a printout of every score of every rider. You can see very quickly if someone is constantly high on one particular rider or low on another. Judging, like riding, is a neverending learning process. ❚

The Psychology of Competition

DR. TIMMIE POLLACK, PH.D

"Choking" is a problem at all levels of competition. One of the greatest examples is what happened to Dan Jansen at the 1988 Winter Olympics in Calgary. He had just been told that his sister passed away. And what happened? He fell time and time again. All hopes for the gold medal dashed because of the huge pressure to focus, and who could blame him? Most of us probably wouldn't have been able to go on at all after hearing such wretched news. But, there are ways to work through these things.

Choking can happen on a smaller scale: someone says something to you that destroys your confidence, you hear bad news, your horse shies. What can you do to get it together enough to put in a good performance? Many people even choose to eliminate all competitions from their life because it isn't worth the whole mental anguish of being at a show. A little scrap of ribbon isn't worth it for them to overcome all the mental obstacles it takes to get to the show. For many, the thought of choking sucks the fun right out of competition—the fun that used to be there before the choking started. It's one vicious cycle.

The unfortunate thing about choking is that it can, and often does, become a pattern. Every time you get tense, your horse feels your tension and starts doing weird things—perhaps even things he never does at home. This is harder to control because you start to think, "Oh, no, there is something wrong with me." This pattern of constant choking may require lots of time to work through.

What shakes most people up about competition is a thing called "performance anxiety." There are basically two categories of fear: fear of physical injury and fear of emotional injury. In performance anxiety you are dealing primarily with the fear of damaging your self-image. Are you going to look good, or will you make a fool out of yourself, do something really stupid or embarrass yourself, or let someone down? A confident person can make mistakes, sometimes really big mistakes, and be able to brush them off or even laugh. That doesn't mean they don't care; they just realize that part of being human includes the fact that we are not perfect, never have been and never will be. A confident person shows resilience in that she can accept this fact and not beat herself up. She uses the situation to learn from and improve. She knows there is a difference between making a mistake and being a mistake. Self-confidence is essential for performing to be comfortable. It actually can be fun!

Self-confident people are optimistic (see page 83 on The Frustration Trap). What this means is when something happens that is negative, an optimistic person might explain this as being temporary, situational and not personal. The flip side is that when explaining something positive, an optimistic person will believe the cause is permanent, pervasive and personal. By the way, women tend to explain success as resulting from good luck while men tend to explain success as due to their skill. Interesting?

So, what other factors make choking more likely? Any time you push the envelope and move outside your comfort zone, there is potential to choke. Say, if you've been competing at the local level and now you are at the state level, or you've moved up to Third Level for the first time in your life, it's very easy to fall into self-talk like, "What am I doing here? I'm not good enough for this." Again, this type of internal dialogue is probably present in more than just your riding. You really have to "watch your language." What you think directly determines how you feel. A sport psychologist can help you identify any of these negative patterns and teach you how to change them.

One of the riders I worked with before the 1996 Olympics was choking big time! She'd enter her class full of tension. By the end of the ride, her horse was sticking his nose in the air and flipping his head, which you don't normally see in rides at this level. What came out in our work together was that with every little mistake or imperfection, she was getting into some really critical, negative self-talk. This would lead to anger, frustration and feelings of hopelessness. The physical tension couldn't help but interfere. We all know how sensitive our horses are to our emotions. You can't fake it. Once she realized what was happening, we worked to teach her how to use phrases like, "It's okay, let it go," or "Let it go. Go on." The difference in her rides was remarkable with just that one change.

These "thinking habits" can be trained in. For example, when Betsy Steiner teaches, you will hear her say, "It doesn't matter" when a horse or rider doesn't get something right away. She simply will have the rider try again. If it still doesn't happen, it might be time to reassess what's happening. No big deal, no fuss. While in competition, it is a bigger deal; in training, you can work to make this attitude and thought pattern a habit.

If you can't stop choking just by that simple intervention, then the next step is to ask what effect this negative self-talk has on your performance. I'll bet the answer that you come up will be that it's screwing it up. There is a price you pay by not working through your choking. The good and bad news is that what you believe and what you say to yourself will is likely to happen. Bad news if you're a negative thinker, good news if you're a positive thinker.

Take a quiet moment alone before your class to calm your nerves and reflect on your task at hand.

LAST CHANCE PHOTOGRAPHY

It takes time, focused attention and repetition to change old habits into healthy habits. One of the ways to do this with cognitive intervention is to dialog with your negative voice. You can even split into what's called a higher-self (the part of you that knows best) talking with the lower-self (the part that's spouting all the negative garbage). Have a little discussion between the two parts and see where it goes.

If you start to freak, there's another technique you can do off your horse, called thought field therapy (TFT). Theoretically, it works with energy flow in the body using principles of Chinese medicine with acupuncture points and meridians. When you are stressed, or freaked, energy flow is disrupted. By tapping on a few specific acupuncture points while thinking about the situation stressing you, the tension can be dramatically reduced or even eliminated within minutes. This is a fairly new technique that seems very effective with performance anxiety or a high arousal level, so there is much promise. The best way to do this is to consult with a psychologist trained in TFT. She will work with you to discover the specific components of your fears/anxieties and will give you a customized pattern for this treatment. Once you have a pattern, you can apply this technique yourself anywhere.

You can't let things bug you. Tell yourself that you're going to ride as well as you can. You need to focus on the task at hand and not get distracted by negative thoughts. That's an ability that all top athletes have—to stay clear and focused. Olympic Team bronze medalist Michelle Gibson said she believes the most important quality of top riders is the ability to stay focused. That's a hard thing to do. But if you can't, you're not going to make it at the top levels. Even at the lower levels you won't be as consistent. You may have good performances, but the constancy won't be there.

Focusing is more about concentrating on what you're doing, what it takes to make it to your goals, and not getting distracted and pulled into things that are not going to work for you. In some ways it might appear to others that you are rather distant, but single-mindedness can often appear that way. The farther you go, the more you may have to sacrifice—not because you're turning into a snob, but because of time and energy you're going to spend every day at your sport. You just can't go ride a horse five days a week and expect to make it to the Olympics, but you can ride a horse five days a week and do well on one horse.

Focus means that you can think about whatever it's going to take to put in a good performance—and that will differ from person to person. Focus means that you only allow yourself to think positive thoughts—which thoughts are helpful and which are getting in the way? Do not allow distracting or interfering thoughts to be part of your program.

Focus not only on your thoughts, but also which people to let in and which to keep out. One of the tools you need to have while competing is to know who supports you and who doesn't—a frequent problem among competitors. What do you do when people come to watch you? Trainers will have students come and bring friends and family and want to introduce them to you. If you're comfortable meeting people, and some people are, they can shift from being social to getting back to the job very easily, but the more stressed you are, the less you'll welcome this. You are going to get distracted, but focus means being able to shift your focus back to your purpose quickly and not get pulled in different directions. That takes experience and being very clear about your goals and purposes. I've seen trainers get downright rude because they didn't know what else to do when someone brings their mom up to meet them just before they go into a class. Also, if there is someone who affects you so much that as a result you're not going to ride well, ask him or her not to come. It could be your husband, wife or someone else you really love. If you're going to spend all this time, energy and money, you want to set it up so that you do the best you can when you compete. Tactfully ask that person not to come. There are lots of reasons you can give them so their feelings won't be hurt.

The lower your arousal level, the easier it is to shift your attention. Your arousal level will lower with experience and with lower levels of competition. Your arousal level will go up with less experience and higher levels of competition. People who keep a good sense of humor about their riding tend to have a lower arousal level. While their riding is important to them, they aren't taking themselves or the moment so seriously that it interferes with their performance. There is a whole physiological change that happens to your body when you're stressed. The more physically relaxed you are will help you deal with choking. Humor is wonderful. Take the North American Young Riders' Championships: the organizers set it up so that the kids have fun. They're trying to teach them early on that competition can be fun.

Under the stress of competition, most people tend to get more hyper and tense. Some people however, go flat and need something to get them going. While the first kind of rider needs to pull away and go inside in order to stay calm and focused, the second type needs to find something to rouse her and rev her up. That may be interacting with other people, watching others ride or listening to upbeat music. It also helps riders focus better because it gets them away from the thoughts brewing in their heads. One of the riders I worked with got very uptight at shows. She was miserable; she just wanted to get it over with. We tried lots of tactics. (Each rider is an individual, and sometimes it takes some trial and error to find the best intervention.) During her warm up she was so tense. I was running out of ideas so I told her to sing. She started to sing, started laughing; and within minutes Grand Prix rider Merrie Velden, who was also warming up, jumped in and started singing with her. The two of them were riding around the warm-up ring singing "My Guy." I don't know if you'd do that in the Olympic warm-up; maybe you could do it silently!

Everybody is an individual, so find out what works for you. If you are the kind of person who does better talking to people and joking right up until the time you get into the arena, do it. If you're the kind of person whose thoughts get in your way, focus on what's going on outside of you. If you're the kind of person who needs to focus on being calm and quieting yourself, then do that. Olympic skater Michelle Kwan iso-

lates herself during competition. At one meet she had a blanket and a pillow and curled up in one end of the dressing room. Scott Hamilton is apparently very goofy and open, interacting with his fellow skaters. A lot of finding out what works for you is very individual and comes from trial and error. Nothing is wrong with either style. It's all about what works for you.

TIPS AND TECHNIQUES

You must work hard to develop confidence. Keep a positive attitude and learn to use either positive or instructional self-talk. If you have trouble controlling your thoughts, when you hear yourself say negative or overtly critical things, train yourself to say "stop it," then replace it with something more positive and supportive. The mind is like a vacuum. If you take something out you must replace it or something else will pop in. And if it's another negative, it's not going to work any better. So you're actually going to have preplanned positives or something else to focus on. Focus on your horse's ears, or tune into the rhythm or your horse's footsteps. Substitute the negative with the phrase "we can do this," or "feel the rhythm." Know which thoughts, feelings and actions work best for you in competition.

One approach, suggested by sport psychologist James Loehr, is to act the part. Play the role of successful rider just like an actor would. Take on the physical movements and characteristics of someone who is confident: eyes up, chin up, shoulders back—the posture of confidence. Use affirmations as part of your self-talk: I love competing, We are getting better. Affirmations are some of the things Jane Savoie talks about in her marvelous book *That Winning Feeling*. If you can't think of one to use, borrow Saturday Night Live's character, Stuart Smalley's, "I'm good enough, I'm smart enough, and gosh darn it, people like me!" One suggestion that works well with kids is to tell them to pretend they are their favorite riders. Be Nicole Uphoff. Do anything to get your mind off the junk that can get in your head.

When you set goals for competition, set specific performance-related goals as well as the goal to win or score high. Aim for smooth transitions, accurate changes, square halts, etc. You have little control over whether you win or not. There are too many uncontrollable factors: the weather, spooky things, your horse's mood, the judge's mood and other competitors, for example. If you focus on doing well with what you can control—doing your job well—you can go home a success regardless of where the judge places you. And, typically, if all else goes well, focusing on your part typically is what helps you score the best anyway.

Many Olympic athletes, especially those who have problems with distraction, will listen to audio tapes. They could be tapes of affirmations, music that's relaxing or music that puts them in a good frame of mind—getting them into the mental state where they feel good or confident or ready. For some people, the tape is just to avoid distraction. For others, it helps rouse them and gets them moving. Put together a tape of music that you like and that inspires you. Come up with your own theme song. ▋

Tales of a Show Groom

KATHERINE BATESON

Katherine Bateson has been Robert Dover's groom and assistant since 1993. She was his groom and right-hand assistant at the Atlanta Olympics in 1996 as well as at the World Equestrian Games in 1994 and 1998. Originally from England, Katherine moved to the United States at age 12. She started out as a groom at Robert Dover's barn, but when she announced that she was making plans to move back to England to work on her BHS certification, Robert convinced her to work for him full time as his assistant. In addition to her stable management duties, she trains horses and teaches. She moves with Robert each year from his summer barn in New York to his winter barn in Florida.

DAILY ROUTINE AT ROBERT DOVER'S FARM

The day starts early for us. We usually start between 6 and 7AM with the goal to have everything finished by the time Robert arrives to start riding around 9 or so. The horses are watered, the trunks are polished and the stalls are cleaned; I want the barn to be looking as perfect as it can look. The horses are fed hay first; and grain is fed 10 to 15 minutes after for maximum digestion. We start cleaning stalls as the horses are eating. We bed on shavings, pretty deeply bedded and highly banked. We have 14' x 14' and 16' x 16' stalls, so we try to keep them bedded deeply to avoid hock sores and fatigued legs. Our horses work hard so we want them to be as comfortable as we can get them. The water buckets all get emptied and scrubbed as we go through and clean the stalls.

After the horses finish their breakfasts, we start to turn them out. Not every horse goes out though. The subject of turning out is such a heated debate among horsepeople, and I think that when you get a dressage horse so fit, it's very difficult to turn them out successfully. There are so many factors to consider, one being the investment that an owner's made in a top-level horse. The owner has to weigh the risks against the benefits. Some horses are so used to a certain lifestyle that they don't enjoy the turnout sessions—they aren't used to the freedom. Instead, we take them on an hour hack in the afternoon, take them out and hand graze them, or walk them as they are drying. Of course, they get an hour's exercise when we ride them. Our horses do get a lot of time out of their stalls. But, on the other hand, we do have a lot of horses to turn out. In a perfect world, the entire barn would be outside all day. I would love that, but in our imperfect world of show horses, it's just not practical.

The horses that do go are turned out individually and never together because of the kicking hazards. They all go out wearing boots all around with bell boots in front. We like to use the Equisport Heidi boots. They are easy to put on and take off and they wash up well. We also like the Professional's Choice brand bell boots. They are nice and soft and they adjust well to many horses. The horses wear flysheets while they're out if it's sunny, which keeps their coats from bleaching out in the sun, and of course also keeps the flies off. They also wear fly masks. I prefer the Absorbine fly masks that have the ears built in. Royal Riders has a nice flysheet with fly repellent baked into the sheet.

Once we've cleaned and bedded the stalls, we sweep the barn aisle, water the horses and we start the other little stuff. We rake outside the barn, and we dust all the tack trunks. We dust the drapes and the furniture in our little sitting area. We also have a little kitchen and we clean it, organize the tack room and generally keep everything as spotless as we can. We spend so much time keeping things clean because appearance is everything in this sport. You need to keep the quality high in every area from the way you take care of your horses, to stable management, to how you set up your barn. If somebody walks into the barn, it should always look perfect. That's very much a George Morris and Robert Dover philosophy. But it is a very professional philosophy too. Even your own appearance counts—wearing a nice polo shirt that's tucked in, having your boots polished all the time, wearing nice clean breeches and putting your hair up. The whole thing is a package deal. These habits will hold you in good stead when you go to a horse show; it will be like any other day. All of your equipment should be so well maintained you don't have to worry about it. If your tack is spotless every day, it's not a big deal to get ready for a show. Pack up everything and take it with you. If you make every day seem like a show day, then the pressure is lessened.

When Robert arrives, his horse is 100 percent ready. We know what horse he wants because we tend to stick to the same routine every day. Of course, we do have a change every now and then. We'll discuss the schedule before he leaves the night before, or he'll call on the phone if he needs an adjustment. He rides his two Grand Prix horses in the morning because that's when he's fresh and focused. Then he teaches the rest of his students.

I watch Robert while he rides. I help him on the ground giving him advice. Every top rider needs eyes on the ground, and I assist him as much as I can.

The aftercare is very individual for each horse. We try not to wash with shampoo too much because it dries out their coats. We try to avoid hosing them as well.

Instead, we curry them. Only their legs get washed every day with an antifungal shampoo because Florida has bad fungus. We make sure their heads are very clean especially around the ears and bridle area. It's very important that their heads are as clean as can be to avoid fungus and skin infections. We use a soft curry so we can go over all parts of their bodies: legs, face and the back of their ears. Then the horse gets taken out and hand grazed until he's cooled out and happy and fresh again. We put a flysheet as well as bell boots on our horses when we hand graze them.

Occasionally, horses that are in hard work or have a history of leg problems get ice boots on their legs. But, again, everything is tailored individually to the horse. You need to find out what your horse's needs are and structure your routine around that. At our barn we try to give really individualized care to each horse while following the basic rules of good stable management—the horses are cool, happy and stay clean.

In the afternoon, our horses get fed lunch—hay and grain. The equipment gets cleaned before we put it away. Wraps and pads get laundered after each use. We have a washing machine at the barn and a large one at the house, so every night we're doing laundry!

We'll also turn horses out in the afternoon. But sometimes in Florida it gets to the point where it's too hot to put horses out in the afternoon. Up north, the heat isn't so intense, and the horses get turned out each afternoon.

It does seem like we put in a long day, and that's certainly true. On a typical day we're usually done in the barn around 5:30 pm. But on days when the vet or the farrier comes, our days can be longer.

OFF SEASON

We don't really have an off-season per se. I know a lot of the jumper people have a few months where they'll just hack their horses and turn them out. I think that's a harder thing to do with a dressage horse because it's more of a process—the strength building and training. But you do have to be more careful to avoid over-training once a horse is a finished Grand Prix horse. I think your program changes a little then because the horse doesn't need any more of the training that, say, a lower-level horse moving up would need.

Our horses get trained year-round, and obviously we'll have a month here and there that is a little bit less of a workload. Once our horses get to be 13 or 14 years old and they've been doing Grand Prix for a few years, to avoid injuries, we are very careful not to overtrain them. When they aren't showing, they do get let down a bit, get more cardio-vascular work, etc. After a huge show like the Olympics, we do give the horses a couple of months where they don't do a lot—especially it it's an older guy. But if you really let them down, it's too hard to bring them back again. It's hard on them and you. That's really the younger horse's game.

Katherine Bateson keeps Robert Dover's horses "show ready" all the time.

CLIX PHOTOGRAPHY

GROOMING AT HORSE SHOWS

We keep up on all of our show trimming; we don't ever let the horses get fuzzy. Again, it's that whole philosophy of being prepared. The horses are used to the process, and it's not this big horrific thing that all of the sudden they have to be standing having hours of beauty treatments. We do keep them looking show-ready all the time. Any day of the week they could be taken to a show. They are body clipped in the winter, inside of the ears clipped with #40 blades, under the jaw with the #10 blade, and their noses with #40's as well. I like to keep the bridle path small—only as wide as the bridle crownpiece. I always try to keep their legs, from the knees and hocks down, clipped with a #10 blade—especially horses with white legs. If you can keep them clean you'll be able to see all the tendons easier and be able to gauge their health better. I tend to leave the whiskers around the eyes, unless they are super long and look like a big mess.

I clip the top of the tail rather than pull it. I'll use the #40 blade for underneath and then tidy the rest with a #10. I don't go very far down the tailbone. A lot of people go farther, but I go about five or six inches down because I feel that the more tail you can save the better. Start out and clip just a little; you can always take more off. I hold the clippers facing downward moving with the hair growth—almost combing the tail hairs with the clipper blade, stripping the hairs off as I go. Moving against the hair is a sure way to take off too much.

I bang the bottom of the tail. It's nice to keep the tail long, but a lot of horses have broken-off tails, so if I have to do it a little shorter to get it to look fuller, it's not the end of the world. It helps to have someone hold the tail up where the horse would hold his tail naturally as he moves. I prefer to use clippers to bang the tail straight across because it's easier for me than using scissors.

In an ideal world, where we have lots of time, we would pick through, by hand, every tail hair every day. But we usually don't have the time. I love the Cowboy Magic leave-in conditioner because it keeps the tail from tangling and repels dust. I don't like to brush the tails too much because doing so tends to pull out hairs. But sometimes I have to if I'm in a hurry. Mainly we try to keep de-tangler on the tail so brushing isn't needed as frequently. If we run into yellow-tail syndrome, we use a hair dye for gray hair. It's sort of a blue color that you put in and don't rinse out. The tail looks a little blue for a few days, but after a bit it makes the tails sparkling white. We do use the shampoo formulated for gray tails too, but we also dye it.

We keep the horses' manes pulled all the time. We don't wait until they're long to do it. We keep it up. If your horse doesn't like his mane pulled, you can use a clipper blade, off the machine, of course, to pull it. It gives it a nice natural look. Use the blade like a pulling comb. Back comb and pull the hairs with the blade. For horses that don't mind the pulling, I'll pull the mane and leave it four to five stacked fingers long, depending on the horse. Manes that stand up straight are braided down. For stand up manes, we try to pull the hairs underneath instead of on top, and this limits the "Mohawk" mane. It also helps to put hair gel in the mane and braid it over. When you're tacking up your horse, put a damp

A good looking winner. Anky van Grunsven and Bonfire at the 2000 Sydney Olympics.

CLIX PHOTOGRAPHY

towel over his mane and that helps train the hair down. We wet our horse's manes every day when they go out to be ridden to keep the hair laying flat.

BRAIDS

The key to success with really artful braids is to practice, practice, practice, and to keep everything tight and small. I use yarn to make traditional hunter braids—the straight braid with the little bump against the horse's neck. The number of braids amount depends on the horse. On average, I put in between 20 and 30 braids. If you have a horse that has a lot of mane, you've got to put a lot more in. A horse with a really short neck needs more braids to create the optical illusion of a longer neck. With a longer neck, you can get away with fewer. Fat necks usually look better with smaller and more plentiful braids and thin necks benefit from fewer braids.

For nice-looking braids, I use a product called Quic Braid. It is a miracle. You spray it in, and it makes the mane sticky and easy to grip, and the braids come out great. In my braiding kit I have lots of yarn in different colors—black yarn for black manes, brown for chestnut, etc. I use black yarn for gray horses instead of white because the white yarn is too shiny. I have a pulling comb that I've customized and marked off the different sizes of braids that I want—an inch to two inches—depending on the horse. I use a wooden clothespin to hold the mane back. I have a pull through, a seam ripper to remove the braids and a pair of tiny, folding sewing scissors. I don't French braid the forelock because, I'll admit it, I'm uncoordinated. I've tried, but since I can't do it, I just do it in a hunter braid.

THE SHOW

The day is very similar to what it would be at home. Again, we try to keep the same routine for the horse's sake. Horses are very routine oriented, and if you can keep it that way, they will perform better for you. They need to feel as much at home as you can possibly make it. We do all our stable work just like at home. The day before the show we find out what time Robert's ride is because sometimes we have to be there at 3a.m. to get ready for an early start. We braid the horses fresh every day, so I add in an hour for that. The actual tacking up takes half an hour and I try to bathe the horse early in the morning, particularly if he has white socks. I try to stick an extra 15 minutes in there for unscheduled things. Robert gets on to warm up half an hour before his class, so everything needs to be ready.

I like to use Quic Shade highlighter for the horse's muzzles, ears, and around the eyes—everywhere that can use black highlighting. And of course, lots of fly spray—layers of fly spray. A horse that gets attacked by flies is the groom's fault! I make sure that everything on the bridle is polished. I even used to polish the noseband with shoe polish, but I'm not as overexcited as I used to be! However, I do try to go over the gear to make sure everything is clean and as perfect as I can get it. We sew the numbers onto the saddle pads with white thread—even if it's a bridle tag. Even when Robert's schooling, I'll sew it on the saddle pad. It's neater, and the number won't flap or come off. We paint the hooves with linseed oil.

We use more sugar than you can imagine. We always have boxes and boxes of sugarcubes. We feed the horses sugar when we're riding because it stimulates the horse's salivary glands and gets their mouths really moist and foamy. Of course, sugar is for treats and rewards as well. Our horses are completely sugar addicted.

THE GROOMING BOX

If I'm at a big event, like the Olympics or the World Championships, I tend to get a little overexcited, and I'll carry an extra girth and an extra noseband just in case something breaks. Most of the time you are a long way from your stall, so it's not feasible to run back to get a replacement. I always carry a bucket with a whip, fly spray, a towel, sugar, a hoof pick, a hole punch, a bottle of water for Robert and a bag to put the warm-up wraps in.

I keep a hoof pick, a human hairbrush, a short-bristled body brush, a flicker brush, a rubber currycomb, a rubber currying mitt, sugar, fly spray and a mixture of Alpha Kerry bath oil in my grooming kit. Put a tiny bit of the oil in a spray bottle with water it helps put moisture into their coats. I'll also keep a spray bottle of alcohol to cut grime and brace the legs.

After the show, I take out the braids, wash their legs and put everything back right away because I like to have everything done and not think about it. I don't like to come to the barn the next day to see a mess. I try to get as much done as I can stand. Sometimes we do late classes and, of course, we're a little less apt to be so tidy. But it's good to get as much put away and tidied as possible. But most important, I make sure the horses are comfortable and happy, and have lots of bedding and water. ▮

Preparations
for the Show

JANE BROWN

STACEY SHAFFER

Jane Brown is not just an owner. She takes the success and well-being of her horses to heart and oversees their care herself. She is responsible for the huge task of organizing the massive amounts of gear, feed, tack and other equipment needed to show top FEI horses. Jane and her husband, Dick, are strong advocates of the United States Equestrian Team (Dick is chairman of the Finance Committee and treasurer) and of dressage. They are the creators of the famed Dressage at the Club, a show designed to attract sponsors, spectators and top-level competitors; and Fiesta at the Club, a powered-down version of the Dressage at the Club aimed at amateur riders. They are the proud owners of Graf George, Foltaire, Guerido, Numir, Jubilee, Nikolaus, and Metro, all ridden by Guenter Seidel.

I'm behind the scenes, not the competitor. I'm the grunge worker, not the star. It's weird, I know, but I clean muck buckets! Here's the point, we have a nice house and we built it as a weekend home in 1975. Number of horses owned—zero. Now we have six horses, countless amounts of equipment, more laundry than anyone can imagine and a storage unit. Our horses are among our greatest joys in life, but because of them, for us, life has changed. One birthday, instead getting something like a glamorous black satin dress, Dick gave me a commercial washer and dryer to deal with the loads of horse laundry I do. As he has often said, I have a degree in laundry. But this leads me to the basis for one of my preparation philosophies: the basis for show organization: Go clean! And that includes your brushes; who knows what germs travel at horse shows.

Some things remain the same whether you are going to a local show by trailer or flying overseas to an international competition. It doesn't matter if you're planning to compete at the top or go for a single win at a local show: reduce stress and be prepared. In other words, *plan*.

Actually, preparation for the next competition begins when we return from the last. I wash all the buckets, refill all the bottles (fly spray, shampoo, leather cleaner, etc.), and generally tidy things and put them away for use next time. It doesn't do any good to fly around for 20 minutes trying to locate a currycomb! My job is to lessen stress. At the showgrounds, we are there for endless hours,

Keep up your clipping chores as a matter of course.
MOIRA HARRIS

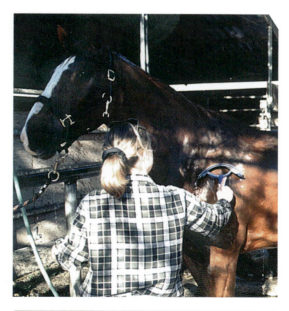

The time to stay tidy is before the show. Don't dart around at the last moment bathing or pulling manes.
LAST CHANCE PHOTOGRAPHY

A USET groom prepares a horse for competition.
CLIX PHOTOGRAPHY

When we used to pack a trunk, George knew show time was near. We learned to hide when doing the packing and made sure George was in his stall, not on the crossties where he could see us. It was said that when the bell rang and Guenter would hold up his hand to begin his freestyle, "smoke would come out of George's ears." We had a show at the Rancho Riding Club and, as the port-a-potties were delivered, Georgie began bucking and leaping. So we always knew that we had to sneak in all the show preparations.

Check all equipment: bridles, saddles, billets, reins, halters, buckets, chains, etc. Make sure they are in good working order and fix them if need be. You may not find an obliging saddler at the last minute! Order feed for the trip, and bags for hay are neater when shipping. For two horses traveling to Europe, I pack two bales of alfalfa, one bale of timothy, plus 200 pounds of grain for a gradual transition to foreign feed. We always have a vet on the receiving end of a trip to check over the horses. Luckily they are good travelers. A groom of ours is always on the plane, even if KLM or FedEx has their own personnel.

I always pack my infamous lists of instructions. Guenter says they are "idiot proof." We usually travel with a different groom from our own at home because Tomas, our at-home groom, has to keep things perfect for "the boys" left at home when we travel. Our travel grooms are super, but helpful advice and direction is always welcome. I never mean to be intimi-

and then suddenly everyone must spring into action before the test. Everything has to be at our fingertips. Simplify your life at a show—even feed can be premeasured in Ziplock bags and, of course, daily vitamins in smaller Ziplock bags.

Fool your four-legged darling. Trim noses, ears and lower legs and bang tails at least a week ahead. Bathe a day or two ahead of departure. I believe that a horse feels your stress and will pick up on it if all of the sudden you start in with the beauty treatments in one fell swoop.

dating but each of our boys is different from the others, and knowing what to expect of them under travel and the stress of competition is beneficial.

Remember that horses feel your stress too. Be extra loving and they will try to give you a first place! ∎

Owners Judith and Steven Bernier show their appreciation for Metallic's hard work.

STACEY SHAFFER

The FEI
Vet Jog

DR. RICHARD MARKELL, DVM

RICHARD MARKELL

Dr. Richard Markell is not your ordinary equine veterinarian. When not completing international passports, conducting prepurchase exams in Europe or attending to his sporthorse practice in Rancho Santa Fe, California, he is officiating at international events as an FEI vet. He was the FEI vet for the 1995 World Cup Dressage Final and treating vet for the 1992 World Cup Show Jumping Final. A 1985 graduate of University of Missouri, Dr. Markell specializes in sporthorse lameness. His long list of clients has included many members of the United States Equestrian Team and several international competitors.

PURPOSE OF THE VETERINARY INSPECTION

There are two purposes for the veterinary inspection. The first is to ensure the well-being of the horse; the jog prevents unacceptably lame horses from competing. The second is to check that the horse presented is the same horse described in the passport. We also review vaccinations and coggins tests listed in the passport. Passports must be correct; inaccuracy can lead to elimination. Most problems encountered during the inspection are incorrect passports, expired vaccinations, and lameness.

HOW TO PRESENT YOURSELF FOR THE VETERINARY INSPECTION

It is your responsibility to ask the show committee when and where the jog will be held. The inspection is conducted by a group of people known as the ground jury, which consists of the judges, the technical delegate, the steward and the FEI veterinarian. This jury has to agree that your horse is sound and passes the requirements of the FEI. It must be a unanimous decision.

FEI rules state that any person responsible for the horse may present him for the jog. However, it is more proper that you, as the rider and competitor, present your horse at the inspection. In respect for the ground jury, you should arrive dressed appropriately (for example, in dress pants and a

❖ OTHER TASKS OF THE *FEI* VETERINARIAN

1. Ensures that the barns are safe.

2. Ensures that the international horses are guarded (for their protection as well as disease control).

3. Consults with the rest of the jury if a horse is to be eliminated.

4. Investigates abuse or excessive spur/whip marks.

5. If a horse becomes ill the FEI veterinarian has to approve the treatment with the show veterinarian. (The FEI veterinarian does not treat horses during the competition.).

The officials are there to help you, not trip you up. Three officials take a moment to "plot."

STACEY SHAFFER

*1. Keep in mind that the FEI
policies on drugs are very different from that
of USA Equestrian. The USA Equestrian's
policy states that responsible medication is in
the horse's best interest. On the other hand,
the FEI believes that no medications are the
best way to go and that a no-drug policy cre-
ates a level playing field. Therefore, no medications of any kind are allowed—no
injectables, no ingestables. The only thing
you may give your horse is food and water.
At a Concours Dressage Internationale
(CDI) event you can't have any needles
(acupuncture needles are allowed), syringes
or drugs in your trunk. And yes, your things
are subject to search at anytime by the FEI
veterinarian.*

*2. Your horse is stabled in a
fenced-off barn which, is under guard at all
times. Only people with credentials or special permission may enter. Even if your
horse is not being shown (say you're only
along for the ride or the only room at the
inn was in the FEI stables), you are still
subject to the jog and passport inspection.
The FEI stable is under international competition rules at all times.*

jacket) with your horse's passport in hand. Your horse should be clean and well turned out and, by tradition, should be braided. Show your horse in hand and in a snaffle bridle. No whips or leg wraps are allowed.

The jog is conducted on a line-up basis, so if you don't want to wait in line or your horse is not fond of standing still, show up early to the inspection. Walk your horse up to the jury, present the passport, and tell them your name and your horse's name. The FEI veterinarian will look at the passport and compare the drawing to the actual horse. Every mark must be described on the drawing. We don't necessarily elimi-nate the riders for missing a mark on their horse's drawing. We do try to help them out with their passports. We'll point out mistakes and suggest that they rectify them as soon as possible. We want our competi-tors to learn this process and to be in line with the rest of the world. When I officiat-ed at the World Cup, I didn't find any inac-curacies in the European passports. Inaccu-racies are not so much the fault of the rider; they are really due to the inexperience of the American veterinarians. It's not that our veterinarians are sloppy; it's that pass-ports are one of the more unusual parts of a veterinarians practice. In Europe, many horses have passports, and passport prepa-ration is a regular part of a European vet-erinarian's practice.

The jogging area will be a level dirt strip about 40 meters long with a marker at the end. Walk your horse one-third of the way, then jog down to the marker, make a right turn around it at the walk, and then jog back. Wait in front of the jury for the deci-sion. They may ask for another jog. If your horse does not pass the jury's inspection at that point, don't worry: you may be given

❖ What's in an Equine Passport?

The equine passport is a red booklet that contains: the identification of the country of origin (where the passport was issued), the owner's identification, certifications of the national federation of the country of origin (for us it's the USA Equestrian), competitions attended, vaccination records, identification of the horse (a drawing of every white mark, scar, cowlick etc. your horse has), medication control (whether he has ever been tested for drugs.), and lab tests (Coggins, etc.).

An equine passport has to be drawn up by a veterinarian and approved by the USA Equestrian. It is required for any and all international competitions. To obtain a passport you need to contact the USA Equestrian and ask for the International Discipline Department. To qualify for an USA Equestrian passport, the horse's owner must be a citizen of the United States. If the owner is not a citizen, they must apply for a passport from his or her country of origin.) USA Equestrian will send you an application for the passport and, if needed, an application for your horse's USA Equestrian lifetime recording which is required to obtain a passport. Return the completed application(s) with the fee for the passport and a fee for the lifetime record. USA Equestrian will send you a blank passport along with FEI guidelines, USA Equestrian tips for filling out the passport and a practice sheet. This practice sheet is included to help your veterinarian get his drawings and markings correct. Mistakes made on the actual passport require White-Out and initialing, and can create a mess. Also, the practice sheet can be faxed to USA Equestrian for approval or suggestions.

Your horse must have two influenza vaccinations recorded on his passport before it can be approved. The vaccinations can be no more than 92 days apart or fewer than 21 days together. So, therefore, count on at least 8 weeks to complete the entire passport process.

If your passport is approved, USA Equestrian stamps it, the secretary signs it and it is returned to you.

---

another chance. If the jury decides your horse is not accepted for competition, they can either accept him with the right to eliminate him at any time if they feel he is not able to continue, or they can give you another chance the next day. When you've passed, your passport gets stamped by the veterinarian with the show's name and returned to you. You're now ready to compete!

Don't let the vet inspection intimidate you. Its role is to protect the horse and to ensure fairness, not to trip up the competitor. The jury is on your side and wants you to be able to compete. ∎

Rider
Turnout

ANNIE McCUTCHEON

Annie McCutcheon originally had a feed and tack store in southern California, but as dressage became more and more popular, the items that riders requested were not available in the United States. Annie felt there must be a national need for all the things that her customers were requesting, and the best place to find these goods was Germany where dressage was as popular as American baseball. They attended trade shows and collected an inventory of goods designed specifically for dressage riders. Today, this collection is compiled into a catalog called Dressage Extensions. Annie knows what's best for her customers. She tests all the goods out on herself, while riding and competing at Fourth Level.

FASHION THROUGH FOURTH LEVEL

At the lower levels you can wear either white or cream-colored breeches. However, the rules specify that you can really wear whatever colored breeches you want, but nobody seems to choose to do so, most stick with tradition. You want to wear a short coat in the dressage style. The dressage coat differs from the hunt coat in that it's longer and has four buttons rather than three. You can choose either a straight-cut style (tapered) or a waistcoat style (cut longer). The proper fit of the waistcoat is one that comes down to the end of your rump. The choice of which style to wear is personal preference, but for someone who is short waisted, the waistcoat is not a good choice because it will be too long, and you'll end up sitting on it. However, the waistcoat is really attractive on tall people. The straight-cut style is a better choice for short-waisted people.

We see all kinds of colors of jackets at the lower levels. I have a brown coat, and I really like it. It's a little bit different, and I always get a lot of nice comments about it. However, mostly what we sell at Dressage Extensions are black and midnight blue coats. That is the preferred, but if you're not afraid to make a fashion statement, choose a color you like. Dressage rider Lynn Roberts wears a green coat with a green hat that really looks pretty. In Germany, several years ago, what was really popular was a burgundy coat. It looked wonderful with a black hat.

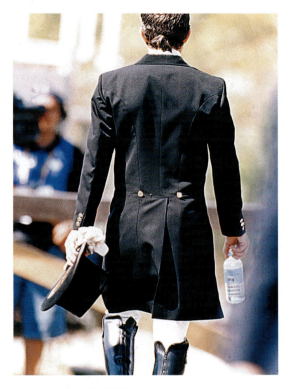

A proper length for the shadbelly is to the back of the knee.

CLIX PHOTOGRAPHY

Most everybody wears a stock tie. It does look nicer, however, you can wear a regular tie or a choker. There are many styles to choose from.

I think that a lot of judges feel that it's appropriate to wear a top hat at Second Level because you're starting collection. More judges prefer to see a derby or a hunt cap at lower levels. The rules won't stop you from wearing a top hat at any level, but most people wait until they are working a higher level of collection.

You can wear either white or black gloves, but if you've got busy hands you are better off sticking with black. The fashion, however, is white, especially from Third Level and up.

FEI Levels

You can make all the fashion statements (within reason) you want at the lower levels, but life gets a bit different as you reach FEI levels. It's a lot stricter, but the rules do allow a short coat, but most people don't wear one at those levels. If you do wear a short coat at FEI, you have to wear a bowler hat, hunt cap or approved safety helmet. At this level, you must wear white or cream-colored breeches.

The shadbelly (or tailcoat), in the past, was cut too short for most people. Today, companies are now making them longer. Pikeur, for instance, is making a longer shadbelly. They have a long/regular and a long/long, which works better for most people. We found that some of the people, who wore a regular in a short coat, were taking a long in the shadbelly. For a proper fitting shadbelly, the tail should come to the bend of the knee. However, this is just the preferred style.

Shadbellys are cut smaller than a short dressage coat so you may want to order the next size up.

Regarding top hats, if you have a long face, you'll want a wider brim with a shorter crown. A round-faced rider should choose a more curled brim and taller crown. Our European hats have the little ribbon hanging off the back. It looks really pretty, and it's quite popular. Nicole Uphoff rides in that hat, and she takes the style with a shorter crown. In North America, traditionally our hats have four-inch crowns. Men's hats have a taller crown, but lots of men don't like the taller hat. Traditionally, all the men used to wear a five-inch crown, but not so much anymore. Most of the hat makers will make any size crown and our Grand Prix hat comes in different crowns. ∎

PART 4

Tips on Riding
Gaits, Paces, and Movements

Collection
and Extension

JEREMY STEINBERG

STACEY SHAFFER

Jeremy Steinberg started out riding a Western gymkhana pony. He switched over to dressage when he and his mother changed boarding facilities, and he never looked back. He won the North American Young Riders' Championship in 1997 aboard Hawkesbury under the tutelage of Dietrich Von Hopffgarten. He trained for a year in Germany before establishing his riding school in Del Mar, California. He now competes very successfully in the open Grand Prix division.

COLLECTION

Collection is the culmination of your training. The whole idea of dressage work is to get your horse to carry more and more weight over his hind legs over a period of time. However, before collection comes, you have to have a solid foundation. I always do everything by the training scale. I start on the bottom and build toward collection. Each step is as important as the previous step, because without the previous step, you can't go on to the next one, and then to the final step—collection.

THE TRAINING SCALE

These criteria are found throughout the whole training process. Since collection begins at Second Level, to begin Second Level, you need to have a basic understanding and applicable comprehension of the training scale. However, collection at Second Level doesn't mean you have "complete" suppleness or "complete" impulsion, etc. From Training Level to Prix St. Georges we are always striving toward these steps. They are idealistic goals, so we can never completely have them.

1. Tempo—the number of footfalls in a set period of time. Tempo should always be established by the rider and is therefore adjustable.

2. Suppleness—This is the basic idea of the rider taking contact on one rein and the horse bringing his head and neck toward that rein and hollowing through his

The collected trot you see at Second Level is a different collected trot from what is seen at Grand Prix. The difference is strength. In a way, collection is a kind of bodybuilding for the dressage horse.

body toward that direction. This is called lateral suppleness.

3. Contact—As the horse accepts the lateral suppleness, he does not have his head up in the air or curled to his chest. Contact refers to a horse that has a basic relaxation in the back and neck and that moves forward toward the bit without fear or apprehension of the rider's hands.

4. Straightening—I say straightening as opposed to straightness because horses are imperfect beings. You can never make a horse perfectly straight, as you could never write as well with your left hand or right hand. So we are always making the horse straighter. The horse needs to be as ambidextrous as possible, but he will never be perfect.

5. Impulsion—Impulsion is thrust or pushing power of the hind legs. It is the idea that the horse pushes himself through the arena instead of pulls with his front legs.

6. Collection—Collection is taking that thrusting power and bringing it farther under the horse's center of gravity, resulting in more upward movement in the entire horse and less ground covering. Again, those thrusting hind legs come farther under the horse, resulting in more engagement of the hind

Piaffe–the ultimate in collection. Christine Traurig and Etienne at the 2000 Olympics in Sydney.

CLIX PHOTOGRAPHY

legs, which, in turn, bend the hip, stifle and hock joints of the horse, lowering the whole croup and, in turn, elevating the front end.

COLLECTION IS NOT...

The myth of collection is that it is to be ridden slowly. If you just slow the horse down, you'll break down the impulsion level in your training scale. In order to have true collection, there must be impulsion. Impulsion is thrust or pushing power of the hind legs. So if we slow the horse down, we are going to lose thrust. Without thrust we have no impulsion and forward energy. Again, collection is shifting energy and balance over the hind legs, never taking it away. Another common fault is to pull the horse's head up to shift his balance backward. However, as your training progresses, you're going to have to start driving the front of the horse up, but still, collection does not mean you can pull on the reins.

Another myth is that the horse's neck must get shorter as the horse gets more collected. The length of the horse's neck never changes from Training Level to Grand Prix. What changes is the actual carriage of the neck out of the horse's shoulder. A horse needs to bring his neck back on his body to help bring weight over his hind legs.

WHAT CHANGES FROM THE WORKING TROT TO THE COLLECTED TROT?

The working gait does not require the horse to swing his hind legs under his body, and the collected gait does. It lacks a certain amount of impulsion and engagement of the hind legs. At the early levels, don't expect to feel a huge difference between working and collected gaits. The difference is going to prove itself in the ability to easily ride the movements that are required, such as shoulder-in or the extended gaits. You also should have a nice flow from one movement to the other. If you try to ride a half pass or medium gait out of a working gait, you're going meet up with some trouble because both of those movements require some degree of collection.

WHAT DOES COLLECTION FEEL LIKE?

If you've ever trotted or galloped a horse uphill, even though it's not collection, that's a feeling toward collection. The horse has to push with his hind legs to get up that hill, and the whole front of the horse grows up in front of you. Collection feels a bit like that. You then have thrust or impulsion from the hind leg and an elevation of the front end.

I think everybody can benefit from having somebody helping from the ground, especially when you're learning what things feel like. Even if you don't have the best assistant, try to get somebody to give you an impression of your ride on a regular basis. It always is best if you can get help from the best. But an educated friend sometimes can be just as much help to give you feedback on how the overall picture looks.

COLLECTION EXERCISES

Shoulder-In: The shoulder-in helps with engagement and impulsion, and straightens the horse, getting the inside hind leg to swing farther underneath the weight of the horse toward his center of gravity.

Ride down the long side and bring the horse's shoulder 30 degrees or so off the wall. Your inside leg stays at the girth and keeps the horse bent around that inside leg and keeps your horse's shoulder from coming in too far. Make sure to turn your shoulders to match the angles of your horse's shoulders.

Caution: The biggest pitfall when riding shoulder-in is that you may get too much angle and you'll have the inside leg crossing over the outside rather than swinging under the horse's body. Try to err on not enough angle rather than too much.

Ten-Meter Circles: The ten-meter circle positions the inside hind leg so that it has to swing underneath the horse's body weight. The farther under that inside hind leg comes, the more engagement you develop. The joints bend, and through that bending you build more hind leg muscles.

Transitions: When the horse halts, he has to step under himself. But, almost more than that, he has to push off from the halt to the trot. Impulsion is basically a development of push from the hind legs resulting in a more engaged hind leg. Make sure your horse responds to your aids quickly with no walking or winding up to the trot.

TYPICAL PROBLEMS THAT COME UP WHEN YOU'RE INTRODUCING COLLECTION

The biggest problem when introducing collection is that the majority of horses here in the United States are not perfectly conformed dressage horses. They don't have big, uphill necks and really nice angu-

Extension is a bigger medium with a larger reach of the front end and stretch of the topline.

lated hind legs, and they don't go in a naturally collected gait like you see in so many of the European horses. That's due to breeding and due to us saying that this kind of horse is what we have and what we want to work with. That's what dressage is here for, after all, to be able to train any horse. However, because of these conformation challenges, tension is the biggest problem encountered when introducing collection.

Tension also appears when collection becomes mentally taxing for a horse. After all, you're asking your horse to work harder than what he'd do in his pasture. However, collection doesn't go against the horse's nature at all, though it should never be forced. But sometimes you may have to encourage your horse to get busy, especially if he's a bit on the lazy side!

If the tension feels momentary, keep working through it. However, if you feel the tension is building, come back to an easier exercise and work your way back up to collection.

EXTENSIONS

There's nothing more beautiful than a lofty, flowing, expressive extension in a dressage test. But on the other hand, there is nothing more painful to watch than a horse scurrying on the forehand in an attempt to extend the gait.

WHAT IS EXTENSION?

There are three different phases of the extended trot: lengthening (encountered at First Level), medium (beginning at Second Level), and extended (found at Third Level and above). Each phase builds on the next as the horse begins to shift his balance uphill. The more collection and strength a horse builds, the bigger your extension will be, relative to your horse's stride. The biggest thing to remember is that the frame and topline of the horse must match his length of stride. As the horse lengthens the frame more and more, there must be a basic idea of collection. If there is not an uphill balance, the horse will fall on the forehand as the extension starts to get bigger.

Note: For the sake of clarity, Jeremy uses the word extension to include all phases.

1. Lengthening comes from a working gait, which, again, means that there is a basic lack of engagement of the hind legs. It's a level and correct balance, but it lacks a certain thrust.

2. Medium gaits build from collected gaits. When you ask for the medium gaits, you'll get more thrust from the hind legs and a bigger movement forward.

3. Extended is a bigger medium with a larger reach of the front end and stretch of the topline.

Christopher Bartle and Wily Trout show off their extended trot.

BOB LANGRISH

EXERCISES FOR EXTENSIONS

Some horses have a natural length-ening, and you won't have to spend a lot of time teaching it; that's great because that's one less thing that you have to do. In general, the average horse isn't like that. Keep in mind that you should be realistic. If your horse doesn't have the biggest stride, extensions are going to take time to develop.

20-METER CIRCLE

For extended work, I take all my horses on a 20-meter circle because I want to stay away from pitfalls like falling on the forehand, running or getting tight in the topline. The circle keeps the horse's inside hind leg engaging. You'll have a little bit of bend, which helps to keep the neck and topline long and stretching. Close your leg

and see what the response is. Does the horse naturally want to run a little bit, or does he lengthen on his own? If your horse responds by rushing, you can do two things:

1. Some horses, even if they have a good length of stride and balance, rush because they don't know what to do. If you keep driving, you can actually push through those rushing strides into some bigger strides. The horse learns that there is more room to move out forward in front of himself.

2. If your horse runs, pulls on the reins, and loses his balance, the first part of our training scale—tempo—has a hole. Go back on your 20-meter circle and establish a quiet gait with a steady tempo, then ask again.

EXTEND AND COLLECT

Your horse needs to learn the difference between extended and collected gaits. To teach him, simply make the collection-to-extension transition many, many times. The stronger a horse gets, the longer he'll be able to hold the extension.

WHAT SHOULD EXTENSIONS LOOK LIKE FROM THE GROUND?

Many times, spectators ooh and ahh over a horse that brings his front legs way up in front in a Hackney-like motion, but that is not necessarily the extension that is required in dressage. The hind legs must match the motion of the front legs. Look for a horse that has level balance, if not an uphill kind of balance. Idealistically, the horse should step over the prints of his front hoof (called tracking up). But, watch where the horse tracks in his collected gait. Some horses, for instance, have a really good active collected trot, but don't always completely track up. The thing to ask yourself is, "Am I building on what nature gave him, or am I taking away?" When the horse that doesn't have a large natural overtrack, starts to over-track in the extended work, you know you are on the right "track."

Collected trot and canter are based on how much bending the three major joints of the hind legs do (the hip, stifle and hocks). In the end, your collection should be presented as a pleasant picture. There should be a basic lightness to a horse's front end the horse should have an easy time getting from, for example, a ten-meter circle to a shoulder-in and from that shoulder-in to straight again. Your extensions will become easier as your collection becomes steadier. ∎

Canter-Walk Transitions

CHARLOTTE BREDAHL-BAKER

COURTESY of CHARLOTTE BREDAHL-BAKER

Born and raised on an island near Copenhagen, Denmark, Charlotte Bredahl-Baker grew up riding everything from draft horses and jumpers to dressage horses. Now a U.S. citizen based in Solvang, California, she has earned her "S" judges rating, won a 1992 U.S. Olympic dressage team bronze medal and ridden her Olympic partner Monsieur and his up-and-coming stablemate Lugano to several United States Dressage Federation Horse of the Year awards. Charlotte began representing the United States in international competition in 1991. She studied with legendary German trainers Conrad Schumacher and the late Herbert Rehbein.

The canter-walk transition shows that your horse has achieved a greater degree of collection compared to what is required at the lower levels. It is a good test of collection because you can't execute a good canter-walk transition unless the horse is in a finer stage of self-carriage. If the horse is not really sitting down on his haunches in good balance, he will fall onto the forehand during the transition or most likely drop into the trot. However, I don't think that the canter-walk itself is as important as the preparation and the exercises for it. Done correctly, these exercises will show that the canter-walk transition is a result of doing your "homework." The canter-walk transition first appears at Second Level as half of the simple change of lead. This simple change is the beginning of teaching your horse flying changes and then, later on the canter pirouette. So rather than thinking of the canter-walk transition as a movement in a test, you should treat it as a basic skill that will help you advance your training.

The canter/walk transitions show that your horse has achieved a great degree of collection compared to what is required at the lower levels. The author on her horse Doubloon.

SHARON FIBELKORN

MISCONCEPTIONS, PROBLEMS AND COMMON MISTAKES

As an "S" judge, the biggest problem I see over and over again is that most riders are unable to collect the canter enough to be able to get from the canter to the walk in balance. I'll see horses that trot into the walk, fall into the walk, stop very abruptly or come against the rider's hand. Most of these problems are due to the fact that the horse is not really collected when the walk is being asked for.

A mistake some riders make is to confuse collection with going slowly. I'll see them slowing down the canter instead of collecting the canter. Changing the tempo (speed) has nothing to do with collection, and will not get a well-balanced walk transition. In fact, during collection the hind legs stay very active and do not slow down. Another common misconception is that some riders think that their horse is being

Canter-walk transitions lead to bigger and better things such as pirouettes.

CLIX PHOTOGRAPHY

disobedient when they have trouble with the transitions. The canter-walk is not just an obedience issue it is a collection and strength issue, which you will address in your daily schooling sessions.

EXERCISES: IS YOUR HORSE READY FOR THE WORK?

Your horse should be solid in his walk-canter transitions before you take on the task of learning canter-walk. Going from walk to canter is easier, and then canter-walk transitions can be taught to your horse at a very early stage in his training. Having walk-canter as a prerequisite to canter-walk will demonstrate that your horse understands the aids for canter and that he can stay round and balanced during the transitions. If your horse still is not able to perform walk-canter transitions fluidly, use the following exercise.

Ride your horse at the walk on a 20-meter circle and ask him to leg yield a few steps away from your inside leg. Make sure your outside leg is slightly back to keep the haunches from swinging out. Immediately after the leg-yield steps, ask for the canter depart. Your horse will be set up well so the depart should be easy for him.

BUILDING BLOCKS

The exercises I do to get really good canter-walk transitions are the same ones I use for the canter-halt and eventually for the canter pirouette. The only difference is increased collection. Ideally, during the canter-walk transitions, the horse is so well engaged that most of the weight is on his hind end. Therefore, the front end is very light, and the horse can make a very soft transition into the walk. The idea is to use exercises that teach the horse collection and help him strengthen his hindquarters.

This exercise is a very basic one that I use frequently. It introduces the horse to collection in the canter, and it works on strengthening the haunches. It also teaches him to "come back," meaning collect, and to go forward out of the collection.

Ride your horse on a 20-meter circle in the working canter. Apply a half halt and ask him to collect for one or two steps. (He should collect when you ask him to but still remain active in his haunches). Then, remaining on the circle, move forward in your working canter. If the horse comes back for one or two steps, be happy with that. In the beginning you don't want to hold collection for very long because your horse will not yet be strong enough. In fact, he'll get unhappy and resistant if you drill for too long or ask for too many steps. Repeat the exercises a few more times, at least every day, about 10 repetitions depending on where your horse is in his training. As your horse gets stronger (when you feel he is sitting more easily) demand more intense collection to the point where he is almost cantering on the spot for a few steps. This is what is known as "school canter." At that moment, don't hold the school canter for long; again, you are building strength. Many times you'll get a loss of energy after the collection as your horse will get a bit tired. In this case, ride medium canter out of the school canter. Ride medium a few steps, collect a few steps and go forward again—back and forth.

STRAIGHTENING OUT

Shoulder-fore in the canter is used to engage the inside hindleg. A lot of horses like to be crooked in the canter and be

The "school canter" is a term for a very collected canter. Not only is it used for transition work, but it also is used for preparation for the canter pirouette. To ride the school canter, half halt on the outside rein and ask the horse to increase his collection. At the same time, use your legs and seat to tell the horse to stay active and to keep cantering. If you don't keep your aids active, he will break to the trot. If he trots because he's trying to avoid collection, tap him with your whip and immediately start again.

What does the school canter feel like? The horse canters with smaller steps and carries much of his weight on his hind end. This gives you the mobility to do just about anything you want. The school canter shouldn't be much slower, and ideally it should be the same as collected canter. If you have no comprehension of what the school canter feels like you may want to have some eyes on the ground. But once you have the feeling—the horse is staying nice and soft and round and active—you shouldn't need much assistance.

slightly haunches-in to avoid carrying themselves. Therefore, it is important to get the inside hind leg to carry more. On the long side of the arena, ask for a slight shoulder-in (shoulder-fore) to make sure that the inside hind is slightly stepping under. This is also a terrific strengthening exercise.

Your horse should be solid in his walk/canter transitions before you take on the task of learning canter/walk.

CRAIG CHANDLER

TIME FOR TRANSITION

When you can finally canter your horse on the spot in school canter, ask for the walk. Because of all your preparation, it will be a simple transition for him. You don't want to practice the canter-walk itself very often because your horse will anticipate the transition and immediately fall into the walk without waiting for your aids. If your horse thinks you are going to keep him cantering on the spot, he will stay active and wait for your aids. Remember, you are starting with a low degree of collection and advancing to a higher degree. This is a very slow process that can take six months to a year depending on the strength of your horse. The truth about canter-walk transitions is that they are really about collection. ∎

Right: As your horse gets stronger you will be able to develop more steps of school canter, a requirement for the pirouette.

CLIX PHOTOGRAPHY

Counter Canter

GERHARD POLITZ

Gerhard Politz, formerly of Stuttgart, Germany, immigrated to Southern California in 1987. He teaches and trains at Flintridge Riding Club near Los Angeles and he travels to other parts of the country to conduct clinics. He holds both the British Horse Society Instructor's License as well as the German Reitlehrer FN. It was in England as a youth were he developed his love for horses, participating in hunting, jumping, eventing and dressage. In his native Germany, he worked with legendary trainers Egon von Neindorff, Gen. Albert Stecken, Willi Schultheis, and Gen. Kurt Albrecht. Gerhard is a USDF Instructor Certification Examiner and he is also a member of the prestigious International Dressage Trainers Club.

In nature, horses very seldom canter on the wrong lead. They'd rather do a flying change to move in a different direction. They may not always do the change cleanly, but counter canter is not something that horses will choose to do in nature. Counter canter is purely a gymnastic exercise that is man-invented, just like shoulder-in and half pass. If a horse happens to do these movements on his own, he does them for only for a very short time. The purpose of the counter canter is to be a gymnastic exercise to help the suppling, balance and collection of the horse.

Occasionally, we might see a horse cantering only on one lead when turned loose. In such a case, I would suspect extreme one-sidedness and stiffness, and in my opinion, it is doubtful that horse will make a good dressage horse.

TERMINOLOGY

Sometimes people use the term counter canter incorrectly. Supposing a rider gives the aids for the right lead canter in a confusing way, the horse strikes off on the left lead. This should not be called counter canter. The horse is simply cantering on the wrong lead. In the counter canter, the horse is asked intentionally to canter on the outside lead versus the inside lead.

PREREQUISITES

When teaching your horse counter canter, it is advisable that he has already learned to go in a somewhat collected canter. The simple fact that you attempt counter-canter, per se, will not collect your horse nor does it straighten him. The horse should also be able to make transitions such as canter-walk-canter without becoming tense.

CORRECT CONCEPT

Many riders go wrong in thinking they have to aid the horse differently when riding counter canter. I think the best advice is very simple: sit and apply the aids exactly like you do on the inside lead, and do not make any changes in your torso as you're going around turns. Just sit quietly and allow yourself to be carried by the horse's movement.

It is definitely a plus if you have a good understanding of shoulder-fore. You should always ride the counter canter in a very slight shoulder-fore—with the leading leg toward the rail—so the exercise has the desired straightening effect. You should also bear that idea in mind when you are riding corners and circles. That's why I think when you have counter canter at the lower levels, as a sort of baby version, you must be very careful at the deepest point of the loop to make sure that the haunches stay straight underneath the horse without falling out of alignment. These early mistakes can haunt you later on if you are not aware of the problem and don't take steps to correct it.

As your horse becomes more balanced in various arena patterns and his collection improves, take care that you work

The purpose of the counter canter is to be a gymnastic exercise to help the supplying, balance and collection.

CLIX PHOTOGRAPHY

toward the same quality of counter canter on both leads. This will further enhance balance and suppleness, which will help you when you school flying changes as your horse's training progresses. Frequently school simple changes (the change of lead through the walk), as this will also improve suppleness and collection.

COMMON MISTAKES

Many mistakes are rider-related, particularly those caused by the rider's seat and position. One frequent mistake is sitting on the wrong seat bone. This becomes particularly obvious when negotiating corners and circles. Instead of being on the inside seat bone (toward the leading leg) the rider hangs behind and throws her horse off balance. Or if the rider attempts to sit on the inside seat bone her shoulders tilt in the wrong direction when going around corners. The rider's torso always should be turned slightly toward the leading leg, and the weight aid is clearly on the inside seat bone. However, be careful not to exaggerate as this may cause you to collapse your inside hip.

Another serious mistake is over-bending the horse's neck. The rider thinks that by exaggerating the neck bend (toward the leading leg) it will prevent the horse from changing leads. That is a big misconception because over-bending the neck actually throws the horse onto the opposite shoulder. For instance, if you're cantering on the left lead and you bend the neck to the left too much, your horse will fall through the right shoulder. When you approach the corner your horse is more likely to lose balance and change in front, or he may trot behind and get totally mixed up.

Another problem originates in overdoing the leg aids, hoping to preserve the counter lead. If the outside leg is brought back too far and with too much pressure, you'll make your horse crooked, contributing to the loss of balance. For example, riding the counter canter in this way pushes the haunches toward the rail and causes the shoulders to come off the rail. This position totally defeats the purpose of counter canter, and you cannot hope to make your horse straight.

Riders who are not balanced themselves tend to make the most mistakes on curves. They don't ride actual curves; the loops turn out rather V-shaped. When you ride three half circles (that's essentially what a three-loop serpentine is), you must consider that the horse should be straight for one or two strides when crossing the centerline before the new loop. But that's not always done. If the rider does not go a few strides straight ahead, the curvature of the loops will be lost, and they will tend to turn out rather like the shape of a V. As a result, when the horse reaches B or E, the haunches fall out and he struggles to keep his balance because of the poor geometry. This is very detrimental to achieving collection. The horse falls onto his shoulders causing him to speed up. Then the rider might half halt the horse and increase the leg aids (mostly with an exaggerated outside leg) in order to prevent the horse from changing leads, which makes him even more crooked. So the inexperienced rider is trying to correct the situation by doing something else wrong.

The horse's outline should remain the same in counter canter as in the true lead, thus showing he is in self-carriage.

SOME USEFUL EXERCISES

As the rider strives for better collection in the counter canter, sometimes the horse may lose impulsion even to the point of losing the rhythm. In this case, freshen up the horse's stride and then collect him again, all in the shoulder-fore. But keep in mind that the shoulder-fore in the canter should be ridden with less angle than in trot. You often see riders over-doing the angle, which actually contributes to the loss of impulsion and purity. The positioning needs to be moderate in order not to stress the horse and to enable him to collect.

Another exercise is to ride a 20-meter circle in counter canter (the best place is in the middle of the arena) and when crossing the centerline, make an outside circle of 15 meters or a 10-meter volte on the inside lead, then return to the original circle in the counter canter. When riding the circle on the inside lead think of shoulder-fore, thus emphasizing the concept of controlling the inside hind leg and outside shoulder. This will help to improve balance and collection when returning to the counter canter circle. But always remember there's no collection without impulsion.

And finally, to prove that your work in counter canter has achieved the desired objectives, i.e. improving balance, straightness, collection and suppleness you should release the reins occasionally *(Uberstreichen)*. The quality of the counter canter should not change, and the horse's outline should remain the same, thus showing that he is in self-carriage. If your horse responds like this, you have done an excellent job. ▮

Shoulder-In and Haunches-In

STEFFEN PETERS

STACEY SHAFFER

German native Steffen Peters turned from the family business to the sport of dressage soon after leaving the army, where he drove a tank. Peters immigrated to the United States in 1985 and became a citizen in 1992. In 1993 and 1998 he broke horses and trained students in San Diego for several years while training his up-and-coming horse Udon. He won the Miller's/USET Grand Prix Reserve Champion at the USET Festival of Champions in Gladstone, New Jersey. Udon and Steffen were memebers of the United States bronze medal winning dressage team at the 1996 Atlanta Olympics. He and his wife, Janet, run a dressage stable in Escondido, California.

When I think about riding a movement, I like to keep it as simple as I can. Sometimes people make up analogies that are extremely complicated. They have to use a certain seat bone more or turn the shoulder more or do this or that with the spine. This kind of explanation is really hard for riders to understand and consequently hard for the horse to understand. To me, shoulder-in and haunches-in are those movements where you should keep proper balance by sitting in the center of the saddle. When the horse turns the shoulders, the rider should sit parallel to the shoulders.

The purpose of every movement in the dressage tests is to help advance the horse to the next level. I personally think that the shoulder-in is one of the most important movements to help the horse through the levels, because the very basic idea of collection is introduced in the shoulder-in. If shoulder-in is done properly, the horse is on his way toward true engagement. And shoulder-in is beneficial, not just in trot, but in walk and canter as well.

Collection means that the horse uses his hip, stifle and hock more than he would in a working gait. And that is exactly what happens in a correctly executed shoulder-in movement. As you ride a shoulder-in, or even the slighter version called shoulder-fore, the horse moves with his inner hind leg a bit more underneath his belly.

As an added benefit, the shoulder-in helps with engaging the horse and it prepares him for straightness.

COMMON FAULTS SEEN AT SHOULDER-IN

The effectiveness of our aids is very important. Many times I'll see a shoulder-in ridden where the rider keeps the inside heel up and the spur stays in the horse. This is a big tip-off that the horse is really not on the rider's aids. A correctly ridden shoulder-in is one where the rider's heel stays down, the outside rein and leg bring the shoulder a little bit in, and the inner rein and leg keep the horse on the rail. I also like to see a rider use a reminding aid before he goes into shoulder-in. He should start with a half halt in the corner, which starts engaging the hind leg.

Once a rider asks for shoulder-in, he should let the horse continue on without constant reminders and support such as the frequent use of the spur or whip. That is what I see too many times. The horse never really has a chance to make a mistake and, consequently, doesn't ever learn to carry the shoulder-in on his own. It's always a good idea to let the horse make a mistake; it helps him learn.

Right: The very basic idea of collection is introduced in the shoulder-in.

CLIX PHOTOGRAPHY

❖ SHOULDER-IN

The difference between a shoulder-in at Second Level and one at Intermediaire I is that the higher level requires more engagement and cadence and shows a higher degree of collection.

Make sure your lateral work is solid before you turn in your entry form.

CLIX PHOTOGRAPHY

In your own schooling sessions, try riding the movement first to see how the horse accepts your shoulder-in aids. If he doesn't react, use a firmer aid to correct him, then see if you can use a little bit of a lighter aid. Your horse will eventually put a little bit more of an effort into the movement and even offer it to you. The object is to make the shoulder-in look effortless and, in fact, that is the goal in all of the movements in dressage.

Another mistake I see often is the one where the horse gets stuck on the rail with the rider unable to turn the shoulders to get the angle. This mistake is also the result of the horse not being on the aids. Often times what has happened is that the rider's become dependent upon using the wall as a replacement to his outside leg. The wall, rather than your leg, is doing the job of stopping the haunches from swinging out. As a result, the horse ignores your leg when you use it. The cure is to take your horse off the rail and ride the shoulder-in on the quarterline or the centerline. You'll wean yourself from the wall and soon learn to rely on your outside leg to keep the haunches in place.

The leg yield is one of the easiest movements to help teach a horse to listen to your outside aids. It also helps the rider check that the horse is on the aids. You can ride the leg yield down the centerline to the wall and from the wall to the centerline. Just make sure that you are riding the leg yield with the proper bend, which would be away from the motion of travel.

Another common mistake is the rider pulling the horse's neck off the rail while leaving the shoulders. The horse has no bend in his body and is doing a "neck-in" rather than a shoulder-in.

Another fault I see is the loss of energy during the shoulder-in. The reason this happens is because in the shoulder-in, it takes a little more effort to engage the haunches. And so sometimes the horse gets the idea to slow down and save a little work on his hind legs. If you're finding that shoulder-in is too difficult for your horse, decrease the angle a little bit and turn it into a shoulder-fore until he's stronger.

SHOULDER-IN AT OTHER GAITS

Shoulder-in at canter is a great exercise to strengthen and straighten the horse. Horses naturally go a little bit crooked more at the canter than in the trot. Keep in mind that the angle is not as acute in the canter as it is in the trot. You can do the shoulder-in at canter on the straightaway as well as on the circle.

You can prepare a flying change and canter pirouette through the shoulder-in. When the horse starts to anticipate and fall against the inner leg during these movements, the shoulder-in is an extremely helpful tool.

Shoulder-in is beneficial for horses that show a little tension in walk, lose the rhythm and even in severe cases, start pacing. The shoulder-in at the walk will give you a good chance to put your leg on your horse without him getting nervous about it. It gives you a chance to say, "Look, get used to it. I'm not trying to bug you, I'm just trying to communicate with you and put my leg on."

HAUNCHES-IN

Haunches-in is the most advanced movement used to teach the horse proper bending to the inside. It's definitely a movement that requires more suppleness, more balance and more rhythm, so make sure your horse is ready for it. In the haunches-in, you'll bend the horse around your inner leg and the horse really starts bending around the ribcage. Because of this increased workload, I see a lot of horses losing the rhythm—much more in the haunches-in position than in shoulder-in position.

The proper position of haunches-in is with the horse's neck and shoulders parallel to the long side with the rest of his body bent to the inside. In other words, if we ride

Once you ask for shoulder-in, let the horse continue without constant reminder.

CLIX PHOTOGRAPHY

haunches-in down the long side, the horse is actually looking at the corner and not to the inside of the arena. There is bend in the neck, but it's not so exaggerated that the horse looks too much to the inside of the arena.

You want to be very picky about your horse accepting the outside leg; that the horse does the movement all by himself and not because there is a spur in his ribs. Your horse needs to move his haunches from your calf. If that doesn't happen, say for a moment he gets a little sticky or decreases the angle, remind him with your outside leg once again, but without getting into that nagging habit.

COMMON MISTAKES SEEN IN THE HAUNCHES-IN

The same mistakes seen in the shoulder-in are often seen in the haunches-in. Again, you need to have a very high standard as to how your horse should react to your aids. Your horse should listen to your aids to increase the angle, the forwardness, the activity and the tempo, and he should carry these through on his own.

Many times, I also see instances, just like in shoulder-in, where the horse's neck is bent way too much to the inside of the arena. If you have difficulty maintaining the correct angle of the hindquarters, start out with a small angle and work up as your horse gets stronger.

If you have the same problems as in the shoulder-in where the horse won't respond to your outside leg, get off the wall and work on the centerline or quarterline. Keep in mind that due to the increased bend, your horse may not be strong enough to do many steps of haunches-in, so mix it up. Do a few steps of haunches-in on the quarterline or centerline, straighten the horse, go back to haunches-in, and straighten the horse again.

If you have trouble maintaining the bend, start the haunches-in from a circle. Use the shape of the circle to create proper bending and then go straight ahead in haunches-in with the same bend you developed in the circle. Repeat the circle if you feel your horse losing the bend. ∎

Half Pass

EVI STRASSER

Evi Strasser emigrated from Germany to Canada in 1988 and became a Canadian citizen in 1994. She was, however, an established rider in her home country, having started lessons at the tender age of 5 at a nearby dressage school and buying her first horse at age 11. On arriving in Canada, Evi worked for Knight & Dawn Stables in Quebec. Evi now runs her own training facility, Good Tyme Stables, and gives clinics in Quebec, Ontario and the United States. Evi and her horse Lavinia represented Canada at their first World Cup Final in 1995 and again in 1997 in The Netherlands. They also competed on the Canadian Dressage Team at the 1996 Olympic Games. She has a young daughter, Tanya.

Champions Nicole Uphoff-Becker and Rembrandt prepare the trot half pass at the 1996 Olympics.

CHARLES MANN

The half pass has held a place in dressage for quite a long time. If you look at the early days of dressage, riders rode their horses in half pass just as they do today. The half pass is a collected movement that is required from Third Level to Grand Prix. It demonstrates that the suppling of the horse has been done correctly and that the horse can move sideways while remaining bent. In lateral work, as you move the horse sideways, the back loosens up. Trainers often request that a rider begin her warm-up in haunches-in and haunches-out. This type of

lateral work helps to relax the back, just as you would stretch your own body. The half pass is the final phase of the lateral work—the top step of the bending hierarchy.

A good half pass is one that shows that the horse is in self-carriage, that the horse keeps a steady rhythm, keeps the flexion and doesn't slow down. Half pass develops from the leg yield and the shoulder-in, building upon these lower level movements. The half pass is also a balancing act. The horse balances his weight on two legs as he crosses his legs over.

As I said earlier, half pass is required from Third Level to the Grand Prix. But the half pass seen at the lower levels is not the same seen at the higher levels. What changes is that in the higher levels the horse has more self-carriage. In the lower levels the half pass may only go to the centerline with less bend and fewer steps. The half pass in the Grand Prix is steeper with more bend, travels a greater distance and moves more sideways. Because the steeper bend is desired and, in fact, needed to get more sideways, more self-carriage is needed. How much more a horse can collect, such as a horse like Anky van Grunsven's Bonfire, adds to how much height a horse can add to the movement. If he's more of a collected horse with higher movement than an extended horse, he can lift a lot in the air. If you have a horse that is more talented at extensions rather than collection, your half passes may not be as high. You need to question what sort of horse you have and don't expect your horse to be equal to a horse that is more collected or extended. Although styles may differ, the same basics remain; you still need to carry your half pass in the same rhythm that you had in the collected trot or canter, keep the bend and move sideways.

You can prepare your horse for half pass by doing several different kinds of lateral work. Haunches-in is good to do because you can control the front end a little better and can get the feel of where the haunches are as in contrast to the front end. Then you can add in your shoulder-in and renvers to be able to move the shoulders as you want. You just sort of move your horse in shoulder-in to haunches-in, etc. Keep in mind that you're not constantly changing directions and movements. If you put everything in one shot together, your horse will be all over the place and he'll be confused. As he advances, you can mix up the steps.

Once you have these exercises very well balanced, start off with a leg yield into the direction you want to go, start your half pass from the shoulder-fore position and move sideways.

I think to get to the point of a good half pass, your shoulder-in has to be very well established because, as I mentioned earlier, the half pass grows out of the leg yield and the shoulder-in. The basic start to a half pass is to begin in a slight shoulder-fore, controlling the movement on the outside rein, engaging the inside hind leg, then moving the horse forward and sideways from the outside rein into the half pass. The rib cage should stay bent as the result of the slight shoulder-fore. The half pass has to come off the outside rein. Half halt, put a

Martina Pracht shows off a gorgeous bend in the trot half pass.

CLIX PHOTOGRAPHY

little pressure on the outside rein, think sideways and bring the horse over into the direction of the half pass.

Review your position as well. You should sit toward the direction your horse is going. That doesn't mean that you should lean in. Continue balancing in the center of the horse. Put more pressure on the inside seat bone. So, for example, if you're moving to the left, put more pressure on the left seat bone.

A common error is when the half pass is correctly moving sideways but the horse is rolled up behind the vertical, which

Christopher Bartle and Wily Trout in canter half pass.

BOB LANGRISH

means he's not through enough in the back to be able to carry enough weight on his haunches. The horse is evading and not listening to your seat and half halts. You have to straighten him and ride more in the direction of his mouth until you feel that you are able to control the hind end to the front end again.

If your horse is the kind who slows down in the half pass, a cure for that is to straighten him and push him sideways into a leg yield, but don't allow your horse to "stutter;" still keep the rhythm. The rhythm has to be like clockwork, and he has to stay "quick." When you've lost your rhythm, you've lost your connection to the front end. When you've got your energy back, move back into the half pass. If your horse is one

of the opposite varieties where he speeds up, halt him, then put him back into the half pass. Make him wait for your aids.

If your horse goes flat with not enough bend so that the half pass resembles a leg yield, the fault lies in the basics. Your horse is probably not bending on the circle or through his body in general. The answer: go back to your basics. You should be able to peel off in a 10-meter circle any time you want with the rhythm remaining the same. If your horse doesn't move sideways, again the fault is in the basics. Your horse is not tuned in to your outside aids. The symptom for this can be noticed while riding your corners. If you have trouble getting out of the corners, you know your horse is not on your outside leg and outside rein—a must for half pass. Move back to your leg yield exercise. Make sure your horse responds very quickly to your outside aids.

Common mistakes occur when the half pass starts with the shoulder falling out so the haunches arrive at the letter before the shoulders do. "Haunches trailing" is often the description judges use for this faulty half pass. The trouble lies in self-carriage. What's happening is that the horse is not bringing his inside hind leg toward the direction of the front end. It also means that the haunches are not carrying. With a lack of self-carriage, the haunches won't carry enough weight. Again, go back to the basics. Go onto the circle and do transitions—halt and trot, upward and downward. You can also repair this through your half pass. When the haunches trail, move onto a small circle and line up the haunches with the front end. Circle, then half pass, and repeat when the haunches trail. Make sure the haunches are engaged. It helps to really try to get a feel where your horse's haunches are when riding the half pass.

Always remember to keep the quality of the gait. It doesn't help you to have your half pass moving sideways, nicely bent, but to have your trot or canter fall apart. Rhythm should stay the same: The trot beats should stay the same and the canter beats should stay the same—always equal. Remember that your basics must not be abandoned when you're moving on. I always stick to the basics from the classical training scale. The basics will help keep you on track. ∎

Flying Changes

JANE WEATHERWAX

STACEY SHAFFER

Jane Weatherwax started riding at a very young age. As a "Navy brat" Jane learned to ride while being relocated to Navy bases all around the world. She would ride anything, and during a stint in Italy was nicknamed "the flea" because she could stick on anything over fences. Today, Jane is a top-level dressage instructor and trainer as well an "S" judge, the highest credential awarded for a dressage judge in the USA Equestrian. She lives in Escondido, California.

When I first started out in dressage, I remember watching a horse do flying changes and I thought they looked like just about the most fun thing a rider could do on a horse. It truly seemed like the horse and rider danced together. More than any other movement we do in dressage, I think most riders look forward to the day when they can ride flying changes themselves. Even to the nonrider, flying changes are fascinating. It's a beautiful thing to watch a 1,000 pound-plus horse skipping like a child. Today, as an "S" judge, I'm certain I must have been watching a very well-trained pair with very correct basics because these changes were so relaxed, straight and expressive without a hint of the rider helping the horse perform them. They appeared to be effortless, and this effortlessness is the hallmark of good flying changes. Indeed, flying changes can be major stumbling blocks for horses on the way up the levels because the strength and carrying of the hindquarters, the acceptance of the rider's aids and confidence all must be firmly established.

THE BASICS

In order to "dance" and perform these beautiful changes, your horse must possess a pure, three-beat, bounding canter to provide the period of suspension needed for the changes to occur. The horse must be straight and through and have an elastic connection through his topline. He must have achieved a certain degree of collection

❖ *SIMPLE CHANGE/SECOND LEVEL REVISITED*

Make sure your horse has a strong grasp of the simple change before beginning to work on flying changes. Simple changes confirm the horse's understanding of the aids of a canter lead and improve uphill balance. They also get the horse through and on the aids and carrying more from behind.

and at least be "thinking" uphill. The rider must ride the quality of the canter before and after the change. Many riders tend to work only on getting a clean change and end up letting the canter lose the quality and forwardness. But also, the horse should have already learned to do counter canter and simple changes of lead through the walk. The horse and rider must know how to change the tempo within the canter itself—to quicken and slow the speed while maintaining the three-beat rhythm. Changing tempo improves the action of the rein going through the topline. Of course, all of this has to be done in relaxation and with confidence. When all of these requirements are fulfilled, you can begin to introduce the changes. Depending on the temperament and conformation of your horse, there are many ways of introducing the flying change.

1. Counter canter circle and change to the inside lead.

2. Half pass to the wall, putting the horse onto the new outside rein and changing.

Good changes are relaxed, straight, and expressive without a hint of the rider helping the horse.

CLIX PHOTOGRAPHY

3. Ride a half circle, then return to the rail in a haunches-in position, and then ask for the change.

4. Ride a figure eight and change in the beginning of the new circle.

THE AIDS

Bring your new inside hip forward a little with your new inside leg coming forward. Then activate your horse and ask for the change with the new outside leg by bringing it back. Keep your upper body straight and keep your seat bones in the saddle. Believe it or not, these aids should be the same aids you use to ask for canter from the walk.

COMMON FAULTS

The most common things that go wrong with the lead changes are usually caused by a lack of one or more of these basics: straightness, suppleness, collection or rider's seat and position.

1. *The horse changing late behind.* The horse often lacks enough forward impulsion or the rider doesn't sit quietly and often lightens his seat, allowing it to come out of the saddle when applying the change aids. Work on your horse's energy and make sure you are sitting quietly when you ask for the change.

2. *The horse changing late in front.* The horse is blocked by the new inside rein being too restrictive and also by a lack of uphill energy. Think about landing in a shoulder-fore.

3. *Swinging of the haunches.* This is caused by the rider moving too much in the saddle with too strong a leg or the horse is bent too much. Fix this by riding forward and quiet your aids.

4. *Croup high with the horse falling on the forehand.* The cause is a loss of confidence and balance. Go back to basics: simple changes and changes in tempo.

5. *Losing the forwardness of the canter.* This loses the period of suspension where the change must occur. The answer is

to energize the horse with your inside seat bone and leg.

6. *Running off after the change.* Again, the horse is losing balance and confidence. Don't pull him up abruptly, but rather, turn him onto a smaller circle to help him regain harmony and balance.

RIDER PREPARATION

The aids for flying changes are the same as the aids for the canter from walk. Sit still, get the horse activated and straight, and work on your horse accepting the new outside rein. Go back to your preparation exercises—simple changes and counter canter.

Try to find where your trouble lies: Is the horse straight and listening to the aids? Be careful not to drill or repeatedly practice the changes when you first introduce them to your horse. Be happy with a few good attempts and reward your horse often. Remember, you must maintain your horse's confidence and relaxation and avoid fatigue—both mental and physical. Above all, never punish your horse for doing the change incorrectly because soon his confi-

Ride the quality of the canter before and after the movement. Ashley Monroe and Kallum at Intermediaire I.

CLIX PHOTOGRAPHY

dence will be lost. A horse's willingness to experiment without fear of punishment is an essential trait that should never be discouraged or lost in your training.

Dos and Don'ts

• Don't ride changes endlessly, or your horse will begin to anticipate the change and mentally fatigue.

• Don't punish your horse for giving you a "dirty" change. You must maintain open communication and promote confidence. You must always reward your horse for trying.

• Do ride simple changes, counter canter and tempo changes within the canter.

• Do praise often with physical and mental breaks for your horse. You'll keep the work interesting and help build his confidence.

• Do sit quietly with your upper body straight and your seat in the saddle with your legs on. Riders who swing or sway take their seat out of the saddle and ride each tempi change with progressively stronger aids. The result is a horse that loses his balance, straightness, confidence and the ability to produce straight changes.

• Do give with your new inside rein so as not to block the new leading inside leg. The horse must feel free to reach more forward with the new inside leg.

• Do put more weight into the new inside seat bone, but don't twist or lean. If you lean, you'll adversely influence the horse's balance and straightness. The forward pushing aid of the weight on the new inside seat bone helps you improve impulsion and energy.

A Word on Tempi Changes

Once a single flying change can be done straight, calm and relaxed, and when and where the rider wants, then "sequence" (or tempi) changes can be introduced.

On the quarterline or eighthline is the best place to start because the closeness to the wall helps with the straightness. First, ask for a change only when the horse feels "through and relaxed." Expressive and straight changes are more important than a correct count of many poor or irregular changes. As long as your horse stays confident and straight you may add another change. Above all, remember that riding forward, keeping the horse straight and staying quiet with your aids will always improve the quality of the changes.

If things go wrong, return to the basics—maybe try doing single changes in different parts of the arena or simple changes. Keep the horse confident and mentally relaxed. More often than not, when things go wrong it's because of the rider. Do your best, think about your basics, keep your aids almost invisible and you'll be on the right track. ∎

Right: Bonfire certainly possesses the three-beat bounding canter so necessary for changes to occur.

Pirouettes

ANNE GRIBBONS

STACEY SHAFFER

Born in Sweden, Anne Gribbons has been training and showing horses in the United States since 1972. She has trained 10 of her horses—six of which were USET long-listed—and several students to the FEI levels. Anne was a member of the USET squad at the North American Dressage Championships in 1985 and the World Championships in 1986. In 1994, she was invited to the World Cup U.S. League Finals riding Leonardo II and ended the year in fifth place in the USET Grand Prix standings. She was a member of the Pan Am silver medal team riding Metallic, who she schooled to Grand Prix. Anne is also an USA Equestrian "S" and FEI "I" dressage judge.

CANTER AND WALK

The purpose of the canter pirouette is to show off the product of our training because there is no real purpose for the pirouette other than demonstrating collection. The pirouette is one of the three (the other two being piaffe and passage) ultimate collected movements, and it is the showcase—the crown jewel—of collection.

The pirouette is introduced at Fourth Level, but at that level we are only kidding because nobody gets totally serious about this movement at the introductory stage, and of course, I'm talking about the horse and rider that are learning this movement. The schoolmaster might throw a rider a good pirouette out of kindness, but most of the Fourth Level horses stumble along for awhile.

From a judge's point of view, a perfect pirouette is a pirouette that is well prepared. The preparation appears logical, simple for the horse to follow, and looks like the horse and rider are really speaking the same language. The pirouette itself stays absolutely rhythmical in the canter. It is small enough so that you can see the horse sitting and carrying weight concentrated on his hind legs. It should stay as small as a good walk pirouette, with the horse's hind hooves staying in the center of the circle and the horse's body moving around the periphery. The horse doesn't lose his canter rhythm, doesn't lose his balance, doesn't slow down or speed up, and doesn't fall or tilt onto the inside leg of the rider. He remains on the aids, through the back and lightly positioned in the direction of travel. In other words, in a left pirouette, he looks to the left and is slightly bent to the left.

Now, if you have all those things, and the pirouette starts and finishes in the same spot—meaning that it doesn't overturn, but starts exactly on the right spot and goes straight after that—if you can do all these things, you get a 10!

FAULTS

The most common faults lie in the preparation. The pirouette is the kind of movement that the rider will know that it isn't going to work three or four strides away. You'll know because you'll feel any of the following: your horse not responding to the half halt, blocking in his mouth, back and neck, or not wanting to go in front of your leg. Your horse will tell you several strides ahead of the pirouette that he's not going to play, and a judge may see that you're headed for disaster as well. On occasion a very kind horse will save a rider's skin and make it happen, but that is rare.

Another common fault is that the pirouette may be a little large. Another is if the horse speeds up in the pirouette. Ideally, he should be in exactly the same canter rhythm as he came in, but that doesn't always happen. Horses rush because they aren't balanced, and they substitute the balance for speed. Another fault is that the horse's bend is not sufficient or doesn't real-

A successful pirouette is dependent upon the preparation.

CLIX PHOTOGRAPHY

ly stay maintained to the inside. But all of these are really minor mistakes.

More serious faults stem from the horse hollowing his back and getting above the aids. Although your horse may still canter around in a pirouette, he won't look correct because he's not round or on the bit. Even more serious faults come from the horse losing his rhythm, slowing down and starting to "climb" or get high in his haunches. This dilemma causes the horse to stick to the ground and no longer move in a true canter, or to lose the canter to a trot,

or to lose the whole gait and walk. Some horses change their leads in the middle of the pirouette. It's pretty athletic but it doesn't get you any bonus points. These are all serious faults that will result in a score of four or less.

PIROUETTE PREPARATIONS

Unlike other movements, things don't change in the middle of the pirouette. A successful pirouette is very dependent on the preparation. If your horse is not truly on the aids, in front of the leg with his back up, cantering in a true three beats and supple enough to bend, he isn't going to perform a good pirouette, no matter how many times you practice it. If anything, it will get worse. You also need to make sure the quality of the canter is good. The pirouette is not going to be any better than a bad canter.

Before the horse starts the pirouette, he should know how to canter in place per se. I dislike using the expression "canter in place" because that's a lot to ask, but he should know how to do a school canter and to shorten both his stride and his body and compact his frame. He should also be able to go forward and lengthen, and then come back again when you tell him until he's like a rubber band. You should be able to get him to do that on a circle and on a straight line.

To ask for the pirouette, select your spot and ask the horse with repeated half halts to rock back and take more weight on his haunches. Your horse has to give you that feeling that he will sit more behind so he raises his forehand and lightens it. The feeling is a little bit like sitting uphill with the motor running underneath your seat bones while your horse stays soft in your hands. Your horse should only turn when you ask because some horses get clever and start the pirouette before you ask. If he anticipates, you can kiss the whole thing goodbye because the pirouette is now going to feel like being on a spinning mechanical bull—out of control. Once the horse starts jumping through your inside leg, you have no control over the pirouette. One end will go one way and the other end will go the other way, and you'll end up sitting in the middle. It's always a disaster. Your horse has to wait and let you give him a half halt and wait for the signal to start the pirouette.

Sit on your inside seat bone, put more weight on your inside foot and try to go with him. Most of the control of the pirouette is done with your outside rein and leg. This means that you guard his outside hindquarters with your outside leg and outside rein. The inside aids help to motivate him: your inside leg keeps saying, "keep cantering, keep cantering," and the inside rein maintains that slight bend.

EXERCISES

A way to introduce the pirouette is to do a quarter pirouette on a square—each corner denoting a turn of only two strides and back to the pattern. Some horses do better learning the pirouette on a circle.

The turn in the pirouette.

CLIX PHOTOGRAPHY

Start out cantering in a shoulder-in on a circle, canter two strides and turn a quarter pirouette. Go forward a few strides and add another quarter pirouette. You can also do the same exercise from the haunches-in. But with haunches-in, you have to watch that your horse doesn't take advantage and run through your inside leg, which means that he falls on your inside leg and leg yields sideways without turning.

You can also develop the quarter pirouette from the half pass. Then you can build on this exercise and ride from the half pass to a half pirouette.

Some horses have a horrible time staying engaged and like to flatten out and get sluggish in the pirouette. These horses will have an easier time if you move them on a little bit, then do a transition back. Add the pirouette while he's still in the transition mode, and this will prevent him from slowing down and getting flat.

Another exercise that is beneficial for horses that are normal and easy to ride is to spiral in from a 20-meter circle and start the pirouette as your spiral reaches the dimension of a tiny volte. As soon as the canter gets labored, leg yield out. Refresh the canter and put your horse back out on the spiral again. Then repeat: go back and pressure him a little, and then back out again. As the months go by and your horse's strength develops, you'll be able to increase the requirements.

RIDER ERROR

Certainly one thing that will hinder a horse is if you concentrate your weight on the wrong side of your horse. Then when your horse goes to the left, you get stuck behind on the right. Now the horse has to drag your body along, and this is very difficult for him. If you're already experiencing problems with your horse, you will compound the problem and he'll most likely give up. It's too hard. If your horse has to drag you along with him, he will still lose his enthusiasm.

A common problem for the novice rider is the belief that she can fix problems

with her hands. If she tries to lead the horse with her hands, she will lose the hindquarters and the pirouettes get worse and worse.

THE WALK PIROUETTE

The walk pirouette, except for the gait difference, is ridden exactly the same as the canter pirouette. However, the walk pirouette is also a wonderful exercise, and I use it a lot to help with engagement. It helps the horse understand how to collect from back to front. The walk pirouette isn't very stressful to the horse, but it's very difficult for the rider to keep the horse absolutely on the aids. It's more difficult than the canter pirouette because the horse needs to move in a good, pure walk, while remaining attentive, and staying engaged. The walk pirouette is also much more difficult for a rider to gauge if she's got it right. A canter pirouette can't be faked. If it's bad, it's bad, and the rider knows it. But it can be difficult to tell if you've got a correct walk pirouette. The canter pirouette is easier to feel because there is more motion and impulsion. The walk pirouette is harder to feel because the horse can easily be evasive.

It's not just preparation that makes a walk pirouette. One of the main faults is that it's very easy for the horse to get behind the leg and then when you ask for the pirouette, nothing happens—nobody's home.

I like to do a little exercise to get the horse to connect to the outside rein. Say you're walking a straight line, ride a leg yield to the right for a few strides, or as many strides as it takes so that you start to feel that the horse is beginning to step out to and "fill" the outside rein (the right rein, in this case). As soon as you feel this, ride a couple of strides of half pass to the left still maintaining him in the right rein. Then you'll feel he's right in front of your leg and well connected to your outside rein, and it will really feel like he's moving into the bridle. Continue from that half pass to the half pirouette. It makes the horse a little bit confused and interested in your aids and prevents him from doing the evasive things that horses tend to do in the walk pirouette like jig, try to piaffe, start to overflex, lose their walk rhythm, etc. This exercise keeps them going. There's a lot of waiting going on while they walk because they have to stay engaged, they have to stay small and keep moving forward, and they have to do a complete turn with bend, balance and on the bit. The beauty of a really good walk pirouette is that the horse looks like he's totally fluid; he never stops walking in the correct rhythm, and he just turns around the inside leg and keeps his walk active. That's not a very common thing to see. A good walk pirouette is very rare.

The bottom line for both the walk and canter pirouettes is that you must have

The walk pirouette, except for the gait difference, is ridden exactly like the canter pirouette.

CLIX PHOTOGRAPHY

proper collection, be careful to keep the horse into the outside rein and make sure you sit to the inside so that you follow the horse's body when he turns. ∎

Passage

GUENTER SEIDEL

STACEY SHAFFER

Guenter Seidel started his dressage career by apprenticing with Herta Beck for his German Bereiter qualifications. Shortly after, he entered the army for his required stint of eighteen months. But after his army tour, he traveled to San Diego for a much-needed vacation. But he never went back. His excellent teaching and training skills made him an instant favorite with the southern California crowd and he soon rose up the ranks of elite dressage riders. He competed and won a silver medal at the Pan American Games in 1995. He was a Bronze Medalist at the 1994 U.S. Olympic Festival and won the 1992 Miller'/USET Intermediaire I Championship aboard Numir. He was a member of the United States Bronze Medal team in the Atlanta Olympics aboard Graf George, placing eighth individually, and again on the Bronze Medal team at the 2000 Sydney Olympics on Foltaire.

A good passage, from the judge's standpoint, has to have height; the front legs should be high and bending and the hind legs active. Of course, each horse is an individual, but these are the ingredients for a good passage. Overall, you want to see the lightness and the self-motivation of the horse. Even if the horse is good both behind and in front, if the rider kicks and spurs, the whole picture is skewed. Therefore, all of these things work together to make passage special.

If you don't have the horse correctly through during a walk-trot transition, you won't be able to get passage. So you want to pay attention to little details like this at the beginning. Even if you're riding an upper level horse who already knows his work, make sure to go back and review the transitions from time to time because you can lose them. It's a common thing to move on to training a horse in more advanced things so much that simple transitions get neglected.

Once you have your transitions down, the work will get easier. Because passage is such a collected movement, a horse can very easily go behind the rider's leg, which causes the passage to get labored and flat. If I'm riding a made horse and I have a little problem, I'll go back and ride a walk-trot or canter-walk transition to make sure the horse really responds quickly and through on the aids and stays in front of my leg. So if you are having a problem, see if you can't find the solution through the transitions. In other words, the problems are the same ones found in the transitions—just slowed down.

❖ HOW DO YOU KNOW WHEN THE HORSE IS READY FOR PIAFFE AND PASSAGE?

You feel it. You can even feel it on a young horse when they get excited about something; you can feel the start of the passage. The horse tells you when he's ready for it. You put a little pressure on, and start making the trot a little more cadenced and springy. And all of the sudden you feel that little bit of hesitation and the passage or piaffe comes. The aids to me are no different than the aids for the collected trot. It's just a little bit of a stronger half halt and a request for little more collection.

One of the assets that seals a horse's fate as a Grand Prix dressage horse is his talent for piaffe. Cindy Ishoy on Dakar.

CLIX PHOTOGRAPHY

A steady passage from Christine Traurig and Etienne.

CLIX PHOTOGRAPHY

PIAFFE

The piaffe is correct when it's over the back, light in the rider's hand, correct in the connection and correct in the diagonal foot fall and, as the horse advances, remains steady in one place.

The problems found in passage are also found in piaffe: When you have trouble, chances are the root of the problem lies in the response to the transition. However, what makes piaffe more difficult than pas-

sage is that piaffe remains in one spot. You can be a little forward in the beginning of your training, but eventually piaffe shouldn't travel. Overall, it's easier to get into trouble in piaffe than in passage because the horse can get claustrophobic from staying in one place. It's very easy to get a horse upset, and he may start spinning or rearing. Particularly with a hot horse, you have to be very careful. You have to consider giving him more breaks and helping him to be comfortable before coming back to the piaffe work. You must really listen to your horse and find out when he's comfortable enough to continue.

THE HALF STEPS

Half step work is also called the forward piaffe, in other words, a piaffe that moves. In the half steps, you are still going to have feeling of piaffe; in contrast, the feeling of passage is more of a bounce and jumping forward. Eventually, the more your horse is schooled and advanced, half steps and piaffe will all become one.

Again, the horse will tell you when he is ready to hold the piaffe. As his strength builds, the more he will be able to stay in one place.

Note: I usually start the piaffe work from the saddle, but I think it's a good idea to also start from the ground. It's easier to start in-hand with a nervous horse because it puts less pressure on him.

THE TRANSITION

The piaffe-passage transition is a difficult thing for a horse to master, although there are a lot of horses that do the transitions well naturally. Graf George was one, for example. The horses who have very good natural piaffe and passage transitions are usually the ones in the top 10.

To make the transition, you ride from the piaffe, move out forward and pick up the passage. This is what *should* happen, but a lot of the times, if the piaffe isn't right, the rider gets stuck and can't move forward. If the piaffe is super correct, the rider will be able to move out into the passage cleanly. If all of this is present in the piaffe, the rider will be able to make the transition to passage quite easily. The resulting passage may not the greatest, but the rider will be out of the piaffe and on his way. If the piaffe is incorrect, say created by the rider's hand or is mechanical, or the horse avoids using all the joints, the transition will not be correct. The transition really shows how correct the piaffe work is.

The truth is, just because your horse is talented in piaffe, doesn't necessarily mean that he's through or correct. All your good scores reflect correct training because you don't just have a score on piaffe and passage; you have them on all the transitions. The reason you deserve so many points is because it shows everything about your horse's training. It shows that your horse is really through, balanced and really over the back. Even if the horse has all the talent, he won't get the scores if he's not doing the transitions well.

Piaffe and passage tell everything about your horse's training.

CLIX PHOTOGRAPHY

The best way for you to learn piaffe and passage is to get on a horse that knows how to do them. If you can't find such a horse, try to get someone knowledgeable to watch you and to point out what is right and what is wrong, because it's often difficult to feel these movements, even if you have experience.

And if that person isn't available, go with your gut feeling. If you have to force your horse every day to get a few steps of piaffe, you should know better. You should

I don't think you can make a rule that says that either piaffe or passage must be taught first. It really depends upon the talent of the horse. Although, I think common mistakes, such as if the horse is stiff and not through, show up more in passage than in the collected trot.

know that you're not doing something right. I'm not saying that you can never punish a horse, but you want to be very careful and know what you are doing because you can really make mistakes in your horse's training—mistakes that can't easily be rectified.

Not every horse can do piaffe and passage and you can't really tell from simply looking at a horse's conformation. You may find that a horse with so-so conformation has a great piaffe and passage, or that a horse with wonderful conformation has no talent for them. You won't really know a horse's ability for piaffe or passage until you try it.

The piaffe-passage work becomes easy for the horse once he understands collection and is strong enough and willing enough to do the movements. Willingness is the biggest factor. To keep the horse willing to do such difficult movements is the key ingredient in passage and piaffe. And, after all, that's what the whole game of dressage is all about. We see so many horses who can do great stuff at home with the rider holding the whip, but then they go into the show ring and are unable to do the work. A lot of horses only work when they know there is the whip, but once they know it isn't there, the motivation is gone, and the horse no longer has the desire to work by himself.

The bottom line is, when you have trouble with piaffe and passage, go back to your basics and make sure they are solid. ▌

Source Guide

RIDER OPPORTUNITIES

Communicating for Agriculture Exchange
Program
Box 677
Fergus Falls, MN 56538
(800) 432-3276

Cross Country International
PO Box 1170
Millbrook, NY 12545
(800) 828-8768
Fax: (914) 677-6077
email: xcintl@aol.com

Yorkshire Riding Centre
(Can also be booked through Cross Country International)
Markington,
Harrogate,
N. Yorkshire, England HG3 3PE
Telephone: (011-44) 1765-677-207
Fax: (011-44) 1765-065

INSTRUCTOR CERTIFICATIONS

Certified Horsemanship Association (CHA).

Contact: 5318 Old Bullard Road, Tyler, TX 75703, Phone: (800) 399-0138,
e-mail: horsesafety@aol.com.

Mission: "To test and evaluate riding program staff for risk management skills, teaching ability, horsemanship knowledge and professionalism."

Certifications: English, Western, pack and trail, Therapeutic Riding. Levels 1-4, Master, Assistant and Clinic Instructor.

Test: 5—7 day certification clinic at approved facilities. Includes evaluation of four lessons, participant riding skills, written test and participation in workshops on industry standards, teaching techniques, professionalism, and herd management. Prerequisites: 18 years of age and sufficient experience with horses.

American Riding Instructors' Association

Contact: 28801 Trenton Court, Bonita Springs, FL 34134, Phone: (941) 948-3232,

e-mail: acrip@aria.win.net
Web site: www.riding-instructor.com

Mission: "To recognize and certify outstanding teachers of horseback riding who instruct students in a safe, knowledgeable and professional manner.

Certifications: Three levels of experience in 11 teaching specialties (hunt seat, stock seat, dressage, distance riding, show jumping.)

Test: Evaluation of ability through written, oral and videotaped lesson at one-day test (scheduled in various locations throughout the United States or Canada) or an annual four-day seminar and testing.

Prerequisites: Varies per level. Minimum 18 years and a good foundation of horsemanship.

United States Dressage Federation (USDF)

Contact: Box 6669, Lincoln, NE, 68506-0669, Phone: (402) 434-8550, e-mail: usdressage@navix.net.
Web site: www.usdf.org

Mission: "Certification implies recognition by USDF of the individual's achievement and capabilities … has demonstrated the knowledge and abilities necessary to teach the concepts of dressage and meet specified standards and proficiencies."

Certifications: Training through Second Level and Training through Fourth Level. Participants my take both exams simultaneously. Tested at approved facilities through USDF Group Member Organizations.

Tests: Participants are observed and graded by two or three examiners. Testing includes six sessions: riding, lungeing the horse and rider, teaching and verbal and written exams.

Prerequisites: First-aid certification and a recommended attendance of USDF approved workshops and precertification clinics.

British Horse Society (BHS)

Contact: Training and Education Department, British Horse Society, Stoneleigh Deer Park, Kenilworth, Warwickshire CV8 2XZ, England.
Phone: (01144) 1926-707700.
e-mail enquiry@bhs.org.uk
Web site: www.bhs.org.uk

Mission: The BHS has a long history and tradition and is the UK national governing body for recreational riding and training. It has been in existence for 70 years and is officially recognized in 28 countries.

Certification: Only the Assistant Instructor (AI) certification is available in the United States. Apprenticeship and testing is conducted at Grand Cypress Equestrian Centre in Orlando, Florida and Millbrook Equestrian Centre in Millbrook, New York. Further certification must be obtained overseas.

Tests: AI candidates are tested in three levels, broken into horse care and riding (required test is three phases: dressage, cross country and a three-foot stadium jumping course); and a separate teacher's exam. After the tests, candidates must teach 250 hours at an approved facility or 500 hours at a nonapproved facility to receive certification.

SUGGESTED READING

(Unless otherwise states, all books can be purchased at your local book or tack store.)

The Dressage Competitor's Handbook and *Financing Your Equestrian Activities* by Suzanne Fraser. Available through State Line Tack, Tack in the Box, and Millers, or you can order it directly from Equissentials Press by calling 603-469-3880. Or on the web site: equissentials.com.

Conditioning the Sport Horse by Dr. Hilary Clayton. Contact Sport Horse Publications, 3145 Sandhill Road, Mason, MI 48854-9425.

That Winning Feeling by Jane Savoie published by Trafalgar Square.

Life Strategies: Doing What Works, Doing What Matters by Phillip C. McGraw, Ph.D. published by Hyperion.

Horses are Made to be Horses by Franz Maringer, published by Howell Book House.

General Regulations of the Federation Equestre Internationale, and *The Rules for Dressage Events*, published by the Federation Equestre Internationale

Riding Logic by Wilhelm Museler, published by Arco Publishing.

Prerequisites: Participants must go through a three-month apprenticeship or prep course learning the criteria of BHS with an approved facility or trainer's. They must also have adequate riding ability and horse management skills.

The Complete Training of Horse and Rider and *My Horses My Teachers* by Alois Podhajsky, published by J.A. Allen, Ltd., London.

The Dressage Formula by Erik F. Herbermann, published by J.A. Allen and Co., Ltd., London.

Teaching Exercises: A Manual for Instructors and Riders by Maj. Anders Lindgrens, published by Half Halt Press.

Dressage: A Guidebook for the Road to Success by Alfred Knopfhart, published by Half Halt Press.

The Art of Training: Lessons from a Lifetime with Horses by Hans von Blixen-Finecke, published by Half Halt Press.

The Competitive Edge II: Moving up the Levels by Max Gahwyler, published by Half Halt Press.

Dressage Insights: Excerpts from Experts by Kathy Connelly and Marietta Whittlesey, published by Half Halt Press.

The Ethics and Passions of Dressage by Charles de Kunffy, published by Half Halt Press.

Leslie Webb's video: *Gymnastic Patterns with Leslie Webb* can be ordered from her website: lesliewebb.com or from Dressage Extensions, 27501 Cumberland Road, Tehachapi, CA 93561, phone: 800-541-3708, website: DressageExtensions.com